International Perspectives of Crime Prevention 4

Contributions from the 4ᵗʰ and the 5ᵗʰ Annual International Forum 2010 and 2011 within the German Congress on Crime Prevention

Eds.

Marc Coester and Erich Marks

with contributions from:
Paul Ekblom, Wiebke Steffen, Jürgen Stock, Irvin Waller, Harald Weilnböck

Forum Verlag Godesberg GmbH 2012

Bibliographic information published by the Deutsche Nationalbibliothek

The Deutsche Nationalbibliothek lists this publication in the Deutsche Nationalbibliografie; detailed bibliographic data are available in the Internet at http://dnb.d-nb.de .

Produced by: Books on Demand GmbH, Norderstedt
Printed in Germany

Print layout: Kathrin Geiß

Cover design: Konstantin Megas, Mönchengladbach

ISBN 978-3-942865-00-5 (Printausgabe)
ISBN 978-3-942865-01-2 (eBook)

Content

Introduction

The German Congress on Crime Prevention is an annual event that takes place since 1995 in different German cities and targets all areas of crime prevention: Administration, the health system, youth welfare, the judiciary, churches, local authorities, the media, politics, the police, crime prevention committees, projects, schools, organizations, associations and science. The desired effect is to present and strengthen crime prevention within a broad societal framework. Thus it contributes to crime reduction as well as to the prevention and the reduced risk of becoming a victim as well as fear of crime. The main objectives of the congress are:

1. Presenting and exchanging current and basic questions of crime prevention and its effectiveness.
2. Bringing together partners within the field of crime prevention.
3. Functioning as a forum for the practice, and fostering the exchange of experiences.
4. Helping to get contacts at an international level and to exchange information.
5. Discussing implementation strategies.
6. Developing and disseminating recommendations for practice, politics, administration and research.

Since its foundation the German Congress on Crime Prevention has been opened to an international audience with a growing number of non-German speaking participants joining. Because prevention is more than a national concern and should be focused internationally this step seemed crucial. Bringing together not only German scientists and practitioners but also international experts in crime prevention and therefore developing a transnational forum to foster the exchange of knowledge and experience constitutes the main focus of this approach. To give the international guests a discussion forum, the Annual International Forum within the German Congress on Crime Prevention was established in 2007. For non-German guests this event offers lectures in English language as well as other activities within the German Congress on Crime Prevention that are translated simultaneously. International guests are able to play an active role by presenting poster or displaying information within the exhibition.

Over the next few years we intend to develop this concept further. It is our wish to build an international forum for crime prevention that ensures a competent exchange of ideas, theories and applied approaches.

This fourth edition of "International Perspectives of Crime Prevention" includes the outcomes of both the 4th and 5th Annual International Forum.

The 4th Annual International Forum took place within the 15th German Congress on Crime Prevention on the 10th and 11th of May 2010 in Berlin and gathered together more than 4000 people from the field of crime prevention in Germany and worldwide. The event was presented in special cooperation and organization with the General Assembly of the European Forum for Urban Security (located in Paris, France) and titled „How cities reconcile security and fundamental rights". Well known experts and a broad audience discussed important topics in the fields of Security and Freedom, Fundamental Rights, Immigration, Security Technologies, Involvement of Citizens and Civil Society. The articles from the 4th Annual International Forum come from Irvin Waller, Paul Ekblom and Harald Weilnböck which all presented important topics in Berlin. Also included is a summary of the event from the perspective of the European Forum for Urban Security, the expertise of the German Congress on Crime Prevention by Wiebke Steffen as well as the Berlin Declaration (a report about the key findings of the congress).

The 5th Annual International Forum took place within the 16th German Congress on Crime Prevention on the 30th and 31st of May 2011 in Oldenburg. This event was held in special cooperation with the Federal Criminal Police Office as well as the Federal Office for Information Security and titled „International Cybercrime - Occurrence, Development, Prevention". The contributions include a summary of the Annual International Forum by Jürgen Stock, Vice-President of the Federal Criminal Police Office, as well as the Oldenburg Declaration.

All articles in this book reflect worldwide views on crime prevention as well as the current status, discussion and research in crime prevention from different countries.

We hope to find a broad audience, interested in the upcoming events of the Annual International Forum as well as the German Congress on Crime Prevention. For more information please visit our website at http://www.gcocp.org.

Marc Coester and Erich Marks

Lectures and Documents from the 4th Annual International Forum

Irvin Waller

Convincing governments to invest in prevention: Reducing crime, Protecting victim rights

Mandela said violence can be prevented in his foreword to the landmark World Health Organization Report on Violence and Health in 2002. WHO looked at scientific research on the causes of crime and violence as well as scientific evaluations of the results of innovations to better tackle those causes.

In sum, we have the knowledge to reduce the number of crime victims significantly by 50% or more. The challenge to policy makers is to make the shift from over-reliance on what is expensive and limited in success to a balance between smart law enforcement and smart investments in what reduces crime and violence. Increasingly, policy makers are making that shift because it protects taxpayers and potential crime victims.

Making Science accessible to Mayors and Legislators

I have made this knowledge and the successes accessible to mayors, legislators, and taxpayers in a book written for them, called Less Law, More Order: The Truth about Reducing Crime – now translated into Chinese, French and Spanish with a German version on the way.

I have combined the science with examples of successful programs that show that national and local government could reduce the number of crime victims by 50 per cent or more by shifting from over-reliance on policing and corrections to smart use of police and smart investments in prevention. Incidentally, it protects taxpayers as most investments in prevention based on the scientific knowledge are much more effective and efficient than paying for reaction.

Indeed, my goal is to shift policy on crime from the reactive classic approach focused on punishing and rehabilitating offenders – that is failing victims and citizens - to a positive preventive approach focused on reducing the number of crime victims – that is meeting the needs of potential crime victims and taxpayers.

The book starts from where the US went wrong, what are the scientifically identified causes of interpersonal violence and crime, what has been proven to reduce crime and prevent victimization, and what are the innovative strategies to mobilize agencies such as schools, housing, children and youth services, as well as families and the police to use what is needed where it is needed most.

It is based on the accumulation of social science research from the last four decades that has been brought together by such prestigious organizations as the World Health Organization, the International Centre for Prevention of Crime affiliated with the United Nations and UN Habitat.

From Expensive Reaction to Effective Prevention

The USA in particular has taken the over-reliance and so over expenditures to extremes with mass incarceration holding one in four of all prisoners in the world for a country with only five per cent of the world´s population. Yet its rates of property and violent crime are little different from countries such as Canada or England and Wales who have made moderate use of more police and prisons. While its murder rates is 200% higher than both of those countries.

The good news is there is strong evidence to prove that specific projects which tackle causes of crime before it happens can reduce victimizations from both violent and property crime. So victimization is preventable. Much of this evidence is based ironically on careful experiments undertaken in the last 30 years in the U.S. These experiments focused on reducing the number of young males involved in victimizing by tackling remedies for negative life experiences such as abusive parenting, dropping out of school, and lack of positive role models.

Even the rampant rates of violence against women can be reduced. WHO has identified special courses in school that change male attitudes and so reduce violence against women. In the developing world, training and micro-finance show impressive results as in Lesotho.

There is also good news that when cities and governments follow a basic multi-sector problem solving process that resources are targeted to gaps in services and so to reduced crime. The City of Bogotá is one of those success stories. Efforts by Cape Town show how partial solutions can work.

Harnessing Knowledge to Prevent Crime

But the book has led to much more. The government of the Province of Alberta has invested $500 million in new dollars over three years into a strategy that balances enforcement, treatment and prevention – the three pronged strategy. It is run by SafeCom which is a modern day responsibility centre that co-locates senior officials from five ministries and is mandated to follow a long term strategy to significantly reduce crime and prevent victimization over a ten year period. This strategy is expected to use surveys such as victimization surveys to measure performance.

The Canadian National Crime Prevention Centre has a $70 million a year program to test promising practices – many of these are also identified in Less Law, More Order. It also chose to fund a new Institute for the Prevention of Crime at the University of Ottawa to develop proposals for a national strategy, contract with experts across the world to inform Canadian crime prevention and launch a network of major Canadian cities to implement collaborative and evidence governance strategies. This institute and the network developed Action Briefs for Municipal Stakeholders as a significant tool for cities to plan better and invest smartly which are encouraging more cities to shift their policies in Canada and across the world.

The Spanish version of the book has momentum of its own with legislation based on the book under consideration by the Mexican parliament and two States with comprehensive policies based on the book. The Vice-President of Argentina recently held a meeting to look at application of the book in Argentina. Venezuela that competes with South Africa for levels of violence and lack of investment in proven strategies have begun to look more closely. It is now in French and Chinese with a German version to follow this year.

The Soros Foundation took interest in establishing a violence prevention fund inspired by the conclusions from the various chapters in the book. In 2010, the World Bank began to look at the book together with expertise from leading American crime prevention experts to solve violence in Latin America. My conclusions from that meeting re-emphasize:

- Mandela´s vision that violence is preventable – i.e. governments can reduce significantly the number of victims of violence on the street and in families – over-reliance on reactive strategies is bad for the economy and democracy
- Key to success is a sustained, comprehensive and results oriented approach led at the highest level of government – not just enforcement and courts
- Potential for Successful Return on investment in effective prevention is significant (in reduced numbers of victims and climate of safety - continued growth in expenditures on only reaction depletes economic and human development

They also provide a check list of programs with promise of short and/or long term reductions in violence including:

- Programs addressing parenting such as triple P and public health nurses and addressing youth such as mentoring and youth inclusion projects
- Reducing the availability and harmful use of alcohol, guns and knives
- Neighborhood programs that create or reinforce collective efficacy
- Public health strategies to tackle criminal youth gangs such as Chicago´s Operation Ceasefire (also original Boston project)
- Empowerment of women; and all female police stations
- Restorative justice and victim assistance

From Rhetoric to Implementation: Good Governance

But these programs have to be directed by good governance strategies that are sustained, comprehensive and results oriented. These need a responsibility center at highest level, sustained investment in training, standards and capacity development as well as

3 year action plans with ten year vision. These must be multi-pronged (enforcement, design, social ...) and a portfolio of short and long term investments. They need to be multi-agency problem solving:

- Diagnosis, plan, implementation, evaluation
- Collaborative that brings together key agencies such as schools, social services,
- Engages public
- All orders of government – municipalities have key role to play but require financial and technical support from other orders of government
- Measuring outcomes/results independently of justice processes – egg using victimization surveys, surveys of violence against women, health data (death and injury), costs and consequences of crime

Cost benefit analysis of projects suggests that increasing investment in "effective violence prevention" over a five year period to the equivalent of 10% of current expenditures on enforcement and criminal justice will reduce violence by 50% over a ten year period. Because of the political pressure to react, one strategy is to require every increase in expenditure on reaction to have an equivalent investment on "effective prevention".

Establishing the governance processes at all orders of government requires immediate investment and capacity development – a city of 100,000 will require two trained crime reduction planners – a national government of 10 million will require an initial group of 30-40 exclusive of statistical instruments and analysis.

Conclusion

The rights of citizens not to be victims of crime require national and local governments to get to know the results of scientific analyses of the causes of crime and the results of programs tackling those causes. Less Law, More Order makes this part easy.

Then they must engage in the reforms that shift from expensive over-reliance on reaction to making smart in investments in programs that are effective in reducing the number of crime victims and making our communities safer. Governments concerned about doing it right and protecting taxpayers are making this shift. Victims are taxpayers and they benefit.

Further Reading

Waller, Irvin (2008) Less Law, More Order: The Truth about Reducing Crime, Manor House, see www.irvinwaller.org

World Health Organization (2009) Violence Prevention: The Evidence, Geneva, see www.who.int/violence_injury_prevention/violence/en/

Paul Ekblom

Citizen participation in crime prevention – capturing practice knowledge through the 5Is framework

Introduction[1]

The field of practical crime prevention and community safety is complex. Knowledge of how to undertake the practice well, and how to replicate 'success stories' in new contexts, is vital. But it's challenging to obtain, organise and apply that knowledge (Tilley 1993; Ekblom 2002, 2005, 2011). We can identify several distinct kinds of knowledge relevant to crime prevention[2] practice (Ekblom 2002, 2011):

- *Know crime* – definitions of criminal offences
- *Know-about crime problems* – their patterns, causes, offenders, harmful consequences
- *Know-what works* to reduce crime, in what context, by what causal mechanisms
- *Know-how to put into practice* – how to undertake the 'preventive process' (Ekblom 1988)
- *Know-when to act* – relative to other activities ongoing or planned for the neighbourhood or city
- *Know-where to distribute resources* – in relation to need, demand etc
- *Know-why* – symbolism, values, politics, ethics – if neglected, these factors can wreck a project
- *Know-who to involve and how* – mobilising and working in partnership with other individuals, groups, organisations and communities

Knowing who to involve and how in crime prevention is arguably the most difficult and complex kind of knowledge to gather and apply. In effect we are here talking about the human condition – how individuals, groups and organisations work, or fail to work, together in society – and how to change people's behaviour in line with societal or government goals (e.g. see Home Office 2006). Much of the pervasive implementation failure of crime prevention programmes can be attributed to human involvement issues. These are the subject of this chapter.

The chapter continues by noting that much crime prevention is delivered by third parties – citizens and organisations – rather than professional crime preventers. Given this, our tools for thinking, communicating and acting through and with such parties

[1]   I am grateful to Kate Bowers, Lorraine Gamman and Aiden Sidebottom for comments, and to the UK Arts and Humanities Research Council for funding the case study.

[2]   Hereafter, for brevity, 'crime prevention' includes community safety.

should be of good quality – but unfortunately they are not. Some arguably better tools are suggested – the Conjunction of Criminal Opportunity and the 5Is framework. These are introduced and finally, further elaborated in action in a case study of 'Involvement failure'. The case study describes an attempt to develop and trial a table-clip to prevent bag theft in bars. Although successful on the product design side, the study encountered such a range of difficulties of collaboration with the various stakeholders at every level that the project was overwhelmed, despite such risks being anticipated and determined attempts being made to control them. The final such difficulty encountered was the world economic crisis of 2008, which brought the planned impact evaluation to a halt. This notwithstanding, the experience provided rich material for learning for both implementing crime prevention through the actions of citizens and other third parties in the real world, and for the design of 'resilient evaluations'.

Who delivers crime prevention?

Some crime prevention interventions are *directly* delivered by professional preventers working in the police service (such as patrols or law enforcement), probation (supervision and support of offenders), local government (such as improving street lighting) or youth services (such as summer entertainment programmes or youth centres). However, the majority of preventive effort is delivered *indirectly* by 'civil' organisations and individuals often in their daily routines of work, travel, domestic activity, family life and leisure. Here, the role of the professionals is mostly to mobilise or work in partnership with the civil world. (See also the concept of 'third party policing' – Mazerolle and Ransley 2006.) And even direct implementation may require professional partnerships to share responsibility for addressing problems, and to span divisions of labour to bring together complementary perspectives and resources (Ekblom 2004).

Inadequate tools for thinking, communicating and acting

Given that so much crime prevention is delivered through third parties, it's unfortunate that the key dimension of 'know-who' for practice, delivery and policy has been understated, underdeveloped and under-structured. Consider these 'methods' – the kind we would expect to see brought together on a typical administrative 'shopping list' of preventive actions:

- Police on patrol
- Crime prevention publicity campaign – 'lock it or lose it'
- Installation of security clips in bars to prevent theft of customers' bags
- Outreach activities aimed at bringing young people on streets into youth centres
- Communities That Care (Crow et al. 2004)
- Neighbourhood Watch

These may look superficially equivalent but in fact all involve professionals, citizens and organisations participating in very different ways. The limitations of our ability to describe and distinguish such forms of involvement affect how well we can think, communicate and act in the preventive domain.

One attempt to structure this involvement has emerged within the Problem-Oriented Policing approach – which explicitly recognises the need to identify and mobilise key stakeholders when dealing with persistent crime and disorder problems. The Crime Triangle (Offender, Place, Target/Victim) briefly summarises some of the main causes of criminal events and simultaneously indicates some fundamental approaches to prevention. In more recent formulations (e.g. on www.popcenter.org/about/?p=triangle) the inner triangle of *causes* is surrounded by an outer triangle of people or organisations who can *influence* those causes – thus 'handlers' influence (potential) offenders, 'guardians' targets and 'managers' places. Sampson et al. (2010) have more recently introduced the concept of 'super controllers' – the people or organisations that in turn influence the immediate handlers, guardians and managers. The Crime Triangle as a framework for cause and intervention is usually accompanied by the SARA model of the preventive process – Scanning, Analysis, Response and Assessment (e.g. Clarke and Eck 2003, www.popcenter.org/about/?p=sara).

Elsewhere (e.g. Ekblom 2005, 2006, 2011) I have criticised this twin formulation as 'useful but limited' in handling the messy complexity of crime prevention practice on the ground. There is insufficient detail beyond the first level of slogans; quite distinct processes are lumped together under 'Response', for example; and the underlying theories (such as routine activity theory and rational choice theory) are insufficiently integrated conceptually and terminologically. Moreover, for practitioners and researchers considering making offender-oriented interventions, the Crime Triangle and SARA are explicitly 'not interested'. I have developed an alternative suite that attempts to be more sophisticated, flexible and comprehensive. This includes the *Conjunction of Criminal Opportunity* (Ekblom 2010, 2011, www.designagainstcrime.com/methodology-resources/crime-frameworks/#list-and-description) an integrated model covering 11 causes of criminal events and counterpart families of intervention aimed at interrupting, weakening or diverting those causes; and the *5Is framework* for the model of the preventive process. Both CCO and 5Is have a structured place for all the tiers of human influence covered by the Crime Triangle and SARA respectively.

Better tools?

Conjunction of Criminal Opportunity (CCO)

The causes of criminal events identified by CCO comprise a juxtaposition of 'things' (material target of crime, enclosure, environment) and 'people' (offenders, preventers and promoters). Offenders are covered in much more detail than by the Crime Triangle. Preventers and promoters are roles that people play, that respectively make crime *less* or *more* likely to occur – as such they are of central relevance to the issue of citizen participation in crime prevention.

Preventers can range from dedicated police patrols, to parents controlling their wayward children, to drivers locking their car securely... to designers of secure products and local governments creating entertainment facilities for young people. The preventer concept covers all tiers of involvement including those people acting within the immediate crime situation, and those acting at one level removed (as with 'super-controllers'); but CCO focuses on the former.

Promoters could be the entirely innocent person who provides cover for a robbery by parking their car in the wrong place at the wrong time; the careless person who pushes pizza advertisements through people's front door letter boxes leaving the end hanging out, which in fact advertises that here is a house with nobody at home; the careless motor manufacturer who designs and sells a car which is easy to break into; the shady electronics dealer who re-chips stolen mobile phones; or the criminal fence who buys them from the thief. Preventive interventions often work by adding or mobilising preventers, or by stopping people acting as promoters – better still, converting them to preventers (e.g. from 'person often leaves door unlocked' to 'routinely locks door').

The 5Is framework

5Is (Ekblom 2011; http://5isframework.wordpress.com; www.designagainstcrime.com/methodology-resources/crime-frameworks/#list-and-description; www.beccaria.de/nano.cms/de/5Is/Page/1/) comprises five task streams:

- *Intelligence* Gathering and analysing information and knowledge on crime, its nature, causes and harmful consequences. The purpose is to inform the specification of crime prevention and community safety aims and priorities to be Implemented; the planning and design of the preventive Intervention/s; and the other tasks that follow.

- *Intervention* Designing and planning practical *methods* to realise particular intervention *principles*. These all aim to block, divert or weaken the causes, and attend to risk and protective factors, of *future* criminal events and careers or of wider community safety problems – so the probability of their occurrence, and the harm they cause, is reduced.

- *Implementation* The wider set of practical and managerial tasks required to *realise the plans and designs* for methods of Intervention, and of the other main tasks of the preventive process. Implementation operates at levels ranging from the specific intervention *methods* themselves, to *projects and services* applying sets of methods, to *processes* like recruitment, training or management of 'delivery units' such as a youth centre or an ad hoc project team.

- *Involvement* Tasks specifically focusing on getting *other people and/or agencies*

to understand, accept, and undertake, share or support the tasks, roles and responsibilities of implementing preventive interventions; or to otherwise support such tasks by alleviating constraints, boosting enablers and establishing a receptive climate. Involvement and Implementation should not be viewed as 'first one step, then the other', but as two intertwined streams – the one *people*-focused, the other *task*-focused.

- *Impact* Gathering and presenting evidence of effectiveness and related evaluative information on the outcomes of the preventive action; also covers process evaluation.

5Is is in many respects a second-generation SARA, and its main task streams map readily onto the earlier framework. The most significant difference for present purposes is that the amorphous 'Response' stage of SARA is divided, in 5Is, into the three analytically distinct task streams of Intervention, Implementation and Involvement.

Involvement as just defined connects with the 'preventer and promoter' concepts of CCO. As said, CCO focuses by convention on those people acting (or failing to act) in the immediate crime situation rather than several steps of cause and effect/social influence away, but Involvement covers the full range. (In POP terms it covers 'super-controllers' rather than merely 'guardians, handlers and place managers' – but I regard these heuristic terms and distinctions as rather inflexible because, for example, even place managers may have 'place-manager-managers' on site).

Involvement is the obvious focus for describing, understanding and influencing citizen participation in crime prevention, but in fact, the three 'Response' concepts together enable a much more complete articulation of what is going on. Let's re-examine the 'shopping list' set out above:

- Police on patrol – *professionals Implement the Intervention themselves*
- Crime prevention publicity campaign – *professionals Involve public, who then Implement the Intervention themselves (they buy, fit and operate window locks)*
- Installation of security clips in bars to prevent theft of customers' bags – *designers create Intervention, and Involve others Implementing it: bar managers (installation), customers (usage)*
- Outreach activities to young people on streets – *youth workers Involve (recruit) young people to join in the activities at a youth centre, co-Implementing their own treatment (Intervention)*
- Communities That Care – *CTC professionals mobilise/form partnership with local civil professionals, and together both mobilise citizens and local organisations to Implement Interventions drawn from a 'what works' menu*
- Neighbourhood Watch – *citizens collectively mobilise themselves, to work in partnership with police, to Implement Interventions centring on surveillance*

We can encapsulate the above examples, and in fact articulate the widest range of crime prevention activity in a structured way, by saying that the professionals *Involve* other parties in *Implementing* the *Intervention* or otherwise supporting it.

The reality is even messier than these brief descriptions allow, of course, as will become apparent. The case study that follows illustrates just how messy and complicated. It also shows how further concepts are needed to articulate the practice issues that arise, in order to aid thinking, communication and sharing of knowledge. Accordingly, as the case study unfolds, we go into progressively greater detail on the process of Involvement.

A case of Involvement failure – the Grippa clip evaluation

The issue of failure in crime prevention

Failure is, unfortunately, a pervasive phenomenon in evaluations of crime prevention initiatives (see Ekblom 2011 for a review). Rosenbaum (1986), discussing the problem in evaluations of community crime prevention programmes, did us the necessary but uncomfortable service of distinguishing between three kinds:

- *Theory failure* (where the fundamental idea behind the intervention was wrong);
- *Implementation or programme failure* (where the theory may have been right but the realisation was weak); and
- *Measurement or evaluation failure* (where the intervention may have worked but the evaluation lacked the power to test it).

Learning from failure is obviously an important activity for practitioners, programme managers and theorists alike. Rosenbaum's concepts are a helpful start in this respect, but aren't detailed enough to help evaluators investigate, articulate and transfer useful knowledge to reduce the chances of failure in future initiatives. Bowers and Johnson (2006) usefully identify a range of more detailed failure risks in reviewing implementation issues. They organise them in terms of these headings: lack of experience, theory failure, under-resourcing, high staff turnover, no champion, lack of infrastructure, lack of exit strategy, red tape, slow implementation and displacement. They cross-classify these risks against operational features of preventive schemes: type of scheme, nature of targets, who is implementing (with obvious connections to Involvement) and how intense the scheme is. Finally, they produce a table which summarises empirical experience for each of the 40 combinations. But imposing even more structure can take this approach still further.

5Is offers just such a structure. As a detailed process model for crime prevention (and a ready-made framework for process evaluation) we can use 5Is to ask, of some wholly or partially failed project or programme, where the failure in question happened. Was it at the stage of Intelligence (e.g. failure to obtain valid crime statistics or to

analyse them appropriately)? Intervention (e.g. failure to apply the right theoretical approach to the problem and context, or to select a sufficiently evidence-based method)? Implementation (e.g. failure to install sufficiently robust window locks on houses)? Involvement (as in the illustration that follows)? Or Impact (e.g. insufficient numbers of observations or too short a time period to give sufficient statistical power in an impact evaluation)? Did the failure reside in just one of these tasks, or in how the whole set was brought together?

Of course, 5Is goes into more detail under each of these tasks and allows a correspondingly finer analysis of what went wrong, and hence what needs to be put right next time. Such finer analysis can also pick up elements of what worked *well* even in the context of a wider failure, rather like a sieve filtering ore from base rock (an analogy similar to Pawson's 2006 use of 'gold nuggets'). For example, a burglary project may have had a badly-designed and implemented intervention, but the method of mobilising participants was excellent and innovative and worth salvaging for wider application, while the rest can be discarded or used as an example of what to avoid.

CCO can help here too. For example it can enable our investigation of Intelligence failure to systematically consider which *causes* of crime were misdiagnosed and why. Within Intervention failure it can guide consideration of a failure to apply the right *theory*. And within Implementation failure it can help us be systematic about which *causal mechanisms* (such as deterrence or discouragement) failed to be triggered (Pawson and Tilley 1997; Ekblom 2002, 2011).

The case study

This brings us to the case study of Involvement failure.

If you visit a public bar, cafe or library your bag, if you have one, is at risk of being stolen. Results from the British Crime Survey suggest that people who visit cafes and bars three or more times a week are at more than twice the risk of theft that those who do not (Kershaw, Nicholas and Walker 2008). Diverse attempts have been made to prevent this category of crime but the ones of interest here centre on the design of products – furniture and fittings – to help customers in such places to protect their property. Various items have been designed and tested at the Design Against Crime Research Centre (DACRC). One is the Stop Thief chair (www.stopthiefchair.com), which has two notches on the front of the seat to allow people to hang their bag securely behind their knees. Another – the subject of this case study – is the Grippa Clip (grippaclip.com) – a hinged loop fixed under the table edge for people to hang their bags on. The clip is easy for the legitimate user to operate but difficult for the thief to remove or steal from the bag because of the obvious, intentional hand/arm movements. The hanging bag moreover remains close to the owner's body space and tactile/visual awareness zone. In terms of causal mechanisms, the Grippa clip sought to increase the effort and risk on the part of offenders attempting to unhook bags, and simultaneously empower preventers (the bag owners); in doing so to reduce opportunities for bag theft.

DACRC and UCL Jill Dando Institute of Security and Crime Science collaborated on what was intended to be a thorough design process informed by research and theory, followed by a large-scale and rigorous impact evaluation of the clips on crime. The study was designed in full awareness of the risks of failure (Ekblom and Sidebottom 2007) – the research team was not naive to these issues (all investigators had experienced and in some cases written on implementation failure). Indeed, following a collaboration with a previous company on bar security (Smith et al. 2006) we systematically undertook risk analyses. We also developed a spreadsheet application (CRITIC – Bowers et al. 2010 and see www.grippaclip.com/publications/academic-papers/critics-link-to-spreadsheet-calculator/) to resolve issues of statistical power on the one hand, and the scale and costs of affordable prototype manufacture on the other. Without being too immodest, the clip design was good, the evaluation design was good, but the people and organisations side, initially promising, let us down, despite receiving much close attention. This is how it happened.

1. Providing a reliable impact evaluation of the Grippa Clips required collaboration with a series of pubs/bars in which to implement the clips and monitor their usage. Following negotiations at high level the top management of one major UK chain of bars agreed to let us trial the clips and (with management board approval) to contribute financially to their production. Anticipating risk, the research team immediately attempted to set up a contractual agreement with the company, though legal negotiations became extremely protracted and were never completed.

2. Meetings were held to brief the local managers of around 30 London bars about the project and to secure their understanding and collaboration, get their feedback on the problem of bag theft and document current preventive measures in place. These meetings were very positive, constructive and enthusiastic. In both top and local management meetings, we were careful to emphasise our sensitivity to issues of improving security *without* harming the reputation of individual bars or of the bar company, as safe places for customers to visit.

3. We took the evolving clip designs through several iterations of test and improvement. We first of all trialled them on paper and computer, then as plastic prototypes (3D printing) in workshop 'critique' sessions with bar staff and police. Here, we were attempting to inject an element of 'co-design' (Burns et al. 2006) into the process, particularly with the various stakeholder groups. Police design advisors who attended were very helpful, but somehow the input from the bar managers was surprisingly limited and disappointing.

4. We then installed prototype clips in two bars where customer opinion was assessed and taken into account. This comprised a series of site visits where observations were made and a standardised questionnaire was given out to both clip users and non-users to gain information concerning their perceptions and experiences of using the clips.

5. The last step was to have been to roll out the finalised clips in the full-scale evaluation. The plan was to have clips deployed in 13 trial bars for comparison with 14 carefully-matched controls using police crime figures, staff-captured victim reports and behavioural observations of bag security. Unfortunately we never got this far. Over two years into the project, with the order for 2000 of the production version of the clips finalised and soon to go into the trial bars, the company suddenly broke off negotiations on the contract (which had continued to drag on) and stated that it no longer wished to continue with the collaboration – though it did, very graciously, wish us well. This was at the peak of the global financial crisis and we can only surmise that there was some connection, the company deciding to put a halt on anything which comprised 'non-core business'. We did go back to head office to offer to release them from their moral commitment to the financial input for production costs provided they still allowed us access to the sites in which to install the clips...but this chain was not for turning. And as it turned out, the company did not seem to get into any serious financial difficulty.

We can go over some of these events in more diagnostic detail, using additional concepts of Involvement in particular to draw out and articulate what was going on, to provide both local feedback and generic, transferrable, lessons.

The task of Involvement is further differentiated, within 5Is, into partnership, mobilisation and climate setting.[3]

*   *Partnership* is about sharing responsibility and risk, and pooling resources, for achieving mutual goals (Ekblom 2004, 2011).

*   *Mobilisation* is less symmetrical and covers those common occasions when professional preventers (in police or local government, say) invite, persuade or sometimes order others to take positive preventive action or to desist from activities which promote crime.

*   *Climate-setting* is a more diffuse activity comprising several tasks: explaining or justifying actions; shifting underlying assumptions (for example about responsibility for a crime problem); changing expectations about who can and should be doing something about the crime problem in question; aligning stakeholders and dutyholders to support one another's goals and understand their constraints;

---

[3]   Other Involvement processes – some of which are more relevant to 'social' or 'community' action, include Outreach, Consultation, Demand, Recruitment, Accountability and Cohesion. See Ekblom (2011) and http://5isframework.wordpress.com.

and healing hostile or suspicious relationships between, say, communities and the police which are blocking specific collaborations to prevent crime.

The next section discusses each in turn in the context of the Grippa clip project.

Partnership

Our relations with the bar company constituted, at top level, what we initially believed to be a *partnership*. This under-wrote our usual process of co-designing with the client. Ultimately the partnership failed to deliver and indeed collapsed. In fact, events revealed that it was illusory, based perhaps on differing expectations and unequal commitment and (despite our efforts with the contract) never formalised.

A few months into the project, the company experienced significant sales reductions (possibly connected with a nationwide non-smoking initiative which came into effect in England in July 2007). Many of the top managers were 'let go' and project liaison was passed to more junior, regional management – a lack of *commitment* and a high-level *champion*. Regional managers, although enthusiastic and committed, didn't have the 'clout' (influence) within the company to make things happen, a lack of *capability*. Moreover, they were moved around geographically rather frequently so *continuity* was both difficult to maintain and labour-intensive. But worse was to befall our relationship as the global financial crisis struck, as discussed under 'climate-setting' below.

Mobilisation

What happened with *local* bar managers can best be described under *mobilisation* – in fact what should have been a *joint* mobilisation of bar managers by researchers and company in partnership. Bar managers were, like their regional supervisors, moved round between venues, again giving problems of *continuity*. This meant our original, efficient and effective group briefing had to be supplemented by repeated ad hoc briefings of new bar managers encountered whilst undertaking observation and data collection. (This was partly an unfortunate side-effect of attempting to boost the power of the impact evaluation by expanding the numbers of bars, illustrating a trade-off between avoiding Involvement failure on the one hand, and Impact evaluation/measurement failure on the other – see Bowers et al. 2009.) Moreover our impression was of inefficient *communication* between regional managers and bar managers. And of course the bartender job throughout the world is notorious for rapid employee turnover.

As said, we piloted our near-final prototype clips in two London bars. Here, we found that the public, when interviewed, liked the designs and the concept. But they didn't actually *use* them – a failure, again, of *mobilisation*. Once again, we can 'zoom in' to the concept of mobilisation to unpick what was going on. The mobilisation process can be characterised by the acronym CLAIMED (Ekblom 2011):

- **C**larify crime prevention roles/ tasks that need to be done
- **L**ocate appropriate preventive agents – individuals or organisations
- **A**lert them that they may be causing crime (as promoters) and/or could help prevent it
- **I**nform them about crime problem, its causes and consequences
- **M**otivate them to act as preventers
- **E**mpower them – increase their capacity by briefing, training or equipment
- **D**irect them – via orders, objectives or standards

The roles in question concerned *acting as preventers of theft of bags in bars*. Specific tasks required of these roles, and the relevant agents, included *installing* the clips (bar company and local managers); actually *using* them to protect bags (customers transformed from inadvertent crime *promoters* to *preventers*); and *encouraging use* of the clips (bar staff).

Installation was not a problem, since the research team undertook this for the pilot, and the bar managers were Directed to accept them by regional managers, but in terms of Information, Motivation and Empowerment the clips were in any case designed to be obvious and easy to fix and to avoid causing damage to the tables they were fixed to.

Use did fail however. Over several months of observation very few of the clips indeed were seen to be employed by customers to secure their bags. What caused this? There seemed to be a problem with Alerting and Informing customers on the existence of the clips and what they were for; and Empowering them in terms of making clear how they were to be used.

We had sought to address this by designing the clips to be visible, in two ways. They were mounted at the edge of the table (earlier police-designed 'Chelsea clips' were hidden beneath the table at some distance from the edge, and site visits had indicated they were rarely used). We also opted for a style that could be described as 'bling not blend', giving the clips a bright red coating rather than a plain brass finish that would more closely fit the bar decor.

We also designed some posters (www.grippaclip.com/design-outputs-2/communica-tio-graphics/) but the bar company confined these to the toilets for fear of impacting on the bars' image of safety. In response to the non-use of the clips, and the restriction on posters, we also designed cardboard 'hangers' showing the clips in use – these were intended to dangle from the clips and catch the customers' attention more direct-ly. With all these communications designs we took pains to ensure a proper balance of mobilising the customers without demotivating the company and managers by scaring the customers off. Indeed, in our 'communications designs' we used the concept of 'caring' more than that of overt security.

There was also an issue of Motivation. Customers interviewed generally approved of the concept and liked the designs; but even when aware, many did not use them. Hints emerged about some people being worried they would forget their bags, or that an overt concern with security was 'uncool' amongst one's friends. Moreover, being relaxed is often part of the culture of bars and cafes which is why people often don't prioritise security. We also formed the impression that there was overall some kind of 'behavioural change inertia'. Further possible causes of the lack of self-protection – the discrepancy between knowing that bags were at high risk on the floors of bars and doing something about it – were explored by research team members Sidebottom and Bowers (2010). Hypotheses included alcohol-induced confusion, lack of definitive knowledge of the safest places to stow a bag, limited placement options (addressed by the installation of the clips) and the well-established psychological principle known as the *optimistic bias* (Weinstein 1980): the tendency to underestimate personal risk – 'it will never happen to me.'

Encouraging use was ideally the responsibility of bar management and bartenders. A parallel trial in Barcelona (http://issuu.com/designagainstcrime/docs/6_grippa_bcn_ english_1_) showed bartenders willing and able to prompt customers to use the clips, gently indicating the crime risk to which they were exposed, and how to use the clips to protect their property. Usage was correspondingly greater in the two Spanish bars.

Unfortunately the staff in the London bars did act like their Barcelona counterparts. Causes were not entirely clear but seemed to include *Motivation* issues. Busy bar staff on low pay and likely to move on in a few weeks or months were perhaps not committed to this extra work; in fact, the hangers, which kept being taken off the clips and dropped on the floor by customers, were seen as a positive nuisance and were not replenished. (One could say this was a design flaw. Being easily removable meant customers took the hangers off, had a look but then didn't put them back on and hence pretty soon they were strewn all over the floor. Our eventual design solution to this was to put a bag silhouette on the Grippa clips themselves, simultaneously avoiding the litter problem and bypassing reluctant bar staff.)

Nor were the bar staff adequately *Alerted, Informed and Directed* by local managers (who were not always present) and regional managers. Communication of purpose and necessary action, and supervision within the company, seemed intermittent on this aspect at least. *Empowerment* was also a problem, in that some bar staff had limited use of English, hindering their communication with customers.

Climate-setting

Where does *climate-setting* fit into the picture? Obviously, our belief that we had established a satisfactory climate of understanding and expectation with the top level of the bar company, leading moreover to a partnership, was illusory. The company itself had originally approached *us* to address theft problems at one of their London bars, but the accepting climate did not appear to have durably and thoroughly permeated the whole of the senior management (nor the legal department protractedly working on the contract).

A more cynical view comes from consideration of the company's own operating environment. The company's approach to us had been made at a time of increasing bag theft from bars more generally, and the company itself had been under considerable expectation and pressure from the Metropolitan Police to do something about the problem – to turn from apparent inadvertent crime promoter to active, responsible preventer. Becoming a partner in our research project was perhaps part of that 'something'. London theft rates declined in subsequent years (although a satisfactory explanation was never determined) and the police pressure was directed against other issues and venues. The motivation to collaborate on this project faded away. The removal of the outside pressures meant that the bar company felt free to change direction. What we had believed was a more fundamental joint interest had in fact been no more than two bodies moving in parallel under very different, but temporarily coincident, forces. What we had believed to be *acceptance* of the value of the Grippa clip initiative had been revealed merely to be *compliance* with momentary influences (e.g. Manstead and Hewstone 1996).

The climate of security *within* the bar, co-created by customers, staff and management, was also limited. There seemed to be few expectations by customers that staff should be taking an interest in their security. Nor did bar staff, in their turn, feel that alerting customers to the risks of placing bags in dangerous places was their job (of course that assumes that they knew which places/positions were or were not risky), or that they had any incentives or support from their seniors to go beyond the call of duty, as it were, and become concerned about theft. There were further complications: the bar staff sometimes expressed the worry that customers would respond negatively if someone pointed out the errors of their bag placement behaviour. Interestingly, the bartender-client relationship in the two bars where clips were trialled in Barcelona appeared to be very different to London. In the former, they can sometimes be said almost to 'perform' to customers (quite possibly for tips) – and are likely to be more integrated among them because of the table service. London as we know often lacks in terms of a good service culture, indicating, as ever, the importance of context.

Integration

So far the approach adopted here has been analytic, dissecting out the various differing aspects of Involvement and focusing on the individual roles played by people and organisations in crime prevention. But we should also consider the whole *system* of influence and activity (or inactivity). Certainly from the point of view of attempting to run an experiment, here was a system where any assignment of responsibility and communication about security issues was severely fragmented. The absence of a 'security thread' running through the whole system and subject to consistent management at all levels meant that, while we had considerable influence over aspects of Intelligence, Intervention and Impact evaluation in this study, we lacked it in Involvement of several key players and Implementation of the tasks and roles we had hoped they would undertake.

Hopefully this case study has demonstrated how we can use the 5Is framework and CCO to articulate and explain this apparently ad-hoc and diverse collection of mishaps and failures in the Involvement of individuals and organisations in crime prevention. The diagram below shows how the 5Is concepts used above relate to one another, in progressively more detailed ways.

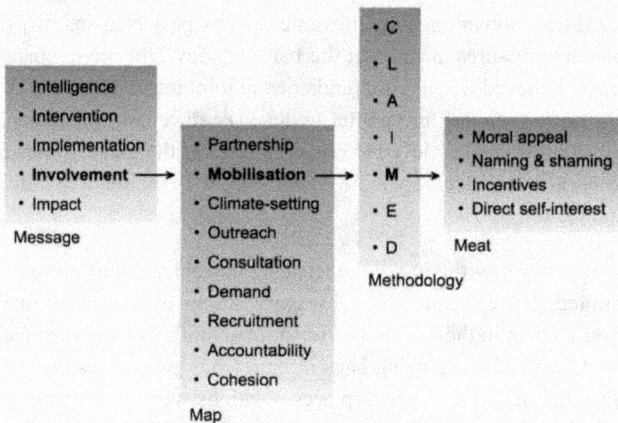

Practical lessons – anticipating, avoiding and addressing Involvement failure

Explanation of Involvement failure, of course, would be of little use if it did not also feed into lessons for both anticipating, avoiding and addressing that failure. Happily, the same tools that diagnose failure can also be used in risk analysis and planning.

On anticipation, risk can be divided into possibility (the undesired events), probability and harm. At the very least, we now have a more detailed and systematic way of identifying generic possibilities of Involvement failure, which can be translated to cover the specific circumstances of the preventive actions that are being planned or are already in operation. An example of this approach in use during the Grippa project was presented by (Ekblom and Sidebottom 2007). Adapting Bowers and Johnson's (2006) approach to classifying and bringing together empirical experience of failures, described above, can build a body of knowledge for anticipating and addressing such risk factors. Combined with a systematic structure like 5Is this could prove very powerful.

On probability and harm, we can reduce the former and prepare for or mitigate the latter by deliberately accumulating articulated practical experience of Involvement failure and the conditions under which it does and doesn't occur. Following Pawson (2006; see also Ekblom 2011) we can attempt to convert this experience into 'middle-range theory' of Involvement processes, and test this in a programme of deliberate experimental *manipulations* of 'Involvement contexts' rather than just research based on interviews and retrospective speculation.

Interestingly, in this last connection DACRC have (at the time of writing) installed Grippa clips (and Stop Thief Chairs – www.stopthiefchair.com) in a busy venue of a major cafe chain and here the Grippas are being used quite readily – perhaps even more so than in the Barcelona bars where they were also tested. Here, then, is a case of *Involvement success*.

But the mere fact of success, though encouraging, is not enough. We need to know what lies behind that success, in a generative way, so we can replicate it in other contexts. What are the physical, cultural, social, organisational and environmental causes underlying the differences in Involvement? What theories do they relate to? How can they be deliberately and acceptably switched on and switched off, as appropriate? How do we get to understand the whole system of use, not just the individual products, procedures and communications in isolation? Certainly the company involved in this new trial is keen to emphasise the commitment of its floor staff to both customers and to the company itself.

More strategically, Cherney (2008) envisages development of a wider 'support delivery system' for crime prevention (organised in terms of 10 Cs!). Another strategic answer may be to design and plan evaluations to maximise *resilience* (a theme I have long pursued – Ekblom 1990, Ekblom and Pease 1995, Ekblom et al., 1997). However, resilience in evaluation can be costly. For example, we considered building redundancy of Involvement into our project by working with more than one company in parallel, and in fact began exploratory negotiations with another. We abandoned this plan however because for one thing, it became difficult to bring the other possible partners to a timely decision, and for another we had by then discovered just how much work was involved in collaborating with one single company and its set of bars.

Another resilience strategy to consider is try to go for shorter, modular projects, where we can 'strike while the iron is hot' and get collaborating companies to act before significant random events derail plans, external pressures upon them to collaborate diminish, and internal changes have time to occur. However, this may conflict with the need to build up adequate research knowledge. The very recent trial of Grippa clips and Stop Thief chairs at a single venue with pre-designed products (as described above) is an instance of this modular approach. However, it does mean the research phase may not so closely relate to and inform the trial phase.

But no matter how we try to build and apply experience and exert influence, involvement will ever remain a complex and risky business. Pawson (2006) takes the view that social interventions always involve the injection of new complexity into existing complex systems. I view these issues in terms of *complex adaptive systems* (Ekblom 2011) with the interventions prone to 'system failure (Chapman 2004). Love (2009) goes further and argues that in crime prevention situations where there are two or more feedback loops the characteristics of successful interventions will probably display counter-intuitive relationships. Humans will almost inevitably get things wrong, unless they are aided by sophisticated system models, preferably dynamic and computerised ones.

Underlying many of the difficulties we experienced in this attempted experiment is the issue of motivation and responsibility, which connects with matters of 'ownership' of problems, governance and even politics. It also connects with climate-setting expectations and norms at the level of national cultures. People in the UK rush to sue the local council when they trip over a loose paving stone – but why don't they think a bar is at least *partly* responsible for their bag going missing when they are on the premises? Experience has shown on car security, and mobile phone security, for example, that even with major 'crime attractors' (Brantingham and Brantingham 2008), significant leverage has to be applied both by police and politically to get people and organisations to change attitudes, expectations and behaviour (e.g. Laycock 2004), including naming and shaming and awakening consumer pressures.

In the final analysis, commitment, communication and continuity of third parties in crime prevention, simply cannot be guaranteed. This is especially true in a changing world with financial crises, local ups and downs of business partners and limited leverage to influence the motivation of people and organisations that one wants to mobilise or engage in partnership. Those damned humans and their complex adaptive systems! But at least we have a start in getting to grips with the issues of citizen participation and related processes, and clarifying how they relate to the other key crime prevention activities of Intervention and Implementation.

References

Bowers, K. and Johnson, S. (2006) 'Implementation Failure and Success: Some Lessons from England', in J. Knutsson and R. Clarke (eds) *Putting Theory to Work: Implementing Situational Prevention and Problem-Oriented Policing.* Crime Prevention Studies 20. Monsey, NY: Criminal Justice Press.

Bowers, K., Sidebottom, A. and Ekblom, P. (2009) 'CRITIC: A Prospective Planning Tool for Crime Prevention Evaluation Designs'. *Crime Prevention and Community Safety* (2009) 11: 48-70.

Brantingham, P. and Brantingham, P. (2008) 'Crime Pattern Theory' in Wortley, R. and Mazerolle, L. (eds) *Environmental Criminology and Crime Analysis.* Cullompton: Willan.

Burns, C., Cottam, H., Vanstone, C. and Winhall, J. (2006) Red Paper 02. *Transformation Design.* London: Design Council.

Chapman, J. (2004) *System Failure: Why Governments Must Learn to Think Differently.* Second Edition. London: Demos.

Cherney, A. (2008) 'Conceptualising a Crime Prevention Support Delivery System'. Paper presented at 21st Australian and NewZealand Society of Criminology Conference, Canberra.

Clarke, R. and J. Eck (2003) *Become a Problem Solving Crime Analyst in 55 Small Steps.* London: Jill Dando Institute, University College London.

Crow, I., France, A., Hacking, S. and Hart, M. (2004) *Does Communities that Care work? An Evaluation of a Community-based Risk Prevention Programme in Three Neighbourhoods.* York: Joseph Rowntree Foundation.

Ekblom, P. (1988) *Getting the Best out of Crime Analysis.* Home Office Crime Prevention Unit Paper 10. London: Home Office.

Ekblom, P. (1990) 'Evaluating Crime Prevention: the Management of Uncertainty.' in Kemp, C (ed), *Current Issues in Criminological Research.* Bristol: Bristol Centre for Criminal Justice.

Ekblom, P. (2002) 'From the Source to the Mainstream is Uphill: The Challenge of Transferring Knowledge of Crime Prevention Through Replication, Innovation and Anticipation', in: N. Tilley (ed) *Analysis for Crime Prevention*, Crime Prevention Studies, 13. Monsey, NY: Criminal Justice Press.

Ekblom, P (2004) 'Shared Responsibilities, Pooled Resources: a Partnership Approach to Crime Prevention', In Ekblom, P. and Wyvekens, A. *A Partnership Approach to Crime Prevention.* Strasbourg: Council of Europe Publishing.

Ekblom, P. (2005) 'The 5Is Framework: Sharing Good Practice in Crime Prevention', in E. Marks, A. Meyer and R. Linssen (eds) *Quality in Crime Prevention.* Hannover: Landespräventionsrat Niedersachsen.

Ekblom, P (2006) 'Good practice? Invest in a Framework!' *Network News,* Spring 2006. Chester: National Community Safety Network.

Ekblom. P. (2010) 'The Conjunction of Criminal Opportunity Theory'. *Sage Encyclope-*

dia of Victimology and Crime Prevention. Thousand Oaks, CA: Sage.

Ekblom, P. (2011) *Crime Prevention, Security and Community Safety Using the 5Is Framework*. Basingstoke: Palgrave Macmillan. See also http://5isframework. wordpress.com.

Ekblom, P., Law, H. and Sutton, M. (1996) *Safer Cities and Domestic Burglary*. Home Office Research Study 164. London: Home Office.

Ekblom, P and Pease, K (1995) 'Evaluating Crime Prevention', in Tonry, M. and Farrington, D. (eds), *Building a Safer Society: Strategic Approaches to Crime Prevention, Crime and Justice* 19:585-662. Chicago: University of Chicago Press.

Ekblom, P. and Sidebottom, A. (2007) 'Managing the risks of evaluating crime prevention interventions using the 5Is framework'. International Crime Science Conference, British Library, London; and International Environmental Criminology and Crime Analysis seminar, UCL, London.

Home Office (2006) Changing behaviour to prevent crime: an incentives-based approach. Home Office Online Report 05/06. http://webarchive.nationalarchives. gov.uk/20110218135832/http://rds.homeoffice.gov.uk/rds/pdfs06/rdsolr0506.pdf

Laycock, G. (2004) The U.K. theft index: an example of government leverage. In Maxfield M. and Clarke, R. (eds) *Understanding and preventing car theft*. Crime Prevention Studies 17. Monsey NY: Criminal Justice Press.

Love, T. (2009) 'Complicated and Complex Crime Prevention and the 2 Feedback Loop Law.' *iDOC'09 International Design Out Crime Conference,* Edith Cowan University, Australia: Design Out Crime Research Centre.

Manstead, S. and Hewstone, M (1996) 'Social influence' in Manstead, S. And Hewstone, M. (eds) The Blackwell encyclopaedia of social psychology. Oxford: Blackwell.

Mazerolle, L. and Ransley, J. (2005) *Third Party Policing*. Cambridge: Cambridge University Press.

Pawson, R. (2006) *Evidence-Based Policy. A Realist Perspective*. London: Sage.

Pawson, R. and Tilley, N. (1997) *Realistic Evaluation*. London: Sage.

Rosenbaum, D. (ed) (1986) *Community Crime Prevention: Does It Work?* London: Sage.

Sampson, R., Eck· J. and Dunham, J. (2010) 'Super controllers and crime prevention: A routine activity explanation of crime prevention success and failure'. *Security Journal* 23: 37-51.

Sidebottom, A. and Bowers, K. (2010) Bag theft in bars: An analysis of relative risk, perceived risk and modus operandi. *Security Journal* 23: 206–224.

Smith, C., Bowers, K. and Johnson, S. (2006). Understanding Theft within Licensed Premises: Identifying Initial Steps Towards Prevention. *Security Journal* 19: 1-19.

Tilley, N. (1993) *After Kirkholt: Theory, Methods and Results of Replication Evaluations*. Crime Prevention Unit Paper 47. London: Home Office.

Weinstein , N. (1980) Unrealistic optimism about future life events. *Journal of Personality and Social Psychology* 39: 806-820.

Harald Weilnböck

'Violence Prevention Network' & 'Cultures Interactive': EU good-practice research on de-radicalisation work in prison and community – and the factor of culture.

With regard to hate crime, Germany's "immigrant society", as is the case in many western countries, faces two major dangers: right wing extremism on the one hand, and religious fundamentalism/ Jihadism on the other. And while the violence is committed by a relatively small number of citizens, extremism and hatred often come from the midst of our societies. For, right wing extremist views do clearly have their roots in the resentments which mainstream societies' harbor against foreigners and other off-stream and disenfranchised groups. And violent actions inspired by a religious fundamentalist world view often show some correspondences to the ordinary religious beliefs and moral attitudes of the respective community. Also, what is true for almost all offenders of these and other forms of extremisms, their acts are determined by micro-social delegations from their families, peer groups and community milieus.

Thus, what the mostly quite young hate crime offenders commit, is, what a significant section of more advanced age-groups of the citizenry sometimes thinks – or sometimes even feels like doing. For sure, this makes the task of effectively dealing with this acute issue not any easier, since the pedagogical attitudes, approaches and methods which are called for in order to prevent and intervene with extremism and hate crime, do not only have to be found and developed – drawing from various sources of societal and scientific knowledge, like pedagogy, social work, sociology, violence studies, psychology/ psycho-therapy – and also cultural studies, dealing with the narratives, factual and fictional, which are ventilated by the media and inspire our worldviews and habits. For, ideally, some base knowledge about the nature of hate crime as well as about the appropriate pedagogical approaches and methods should be shared and supported by what is mainstream consciousness in the society into which the offenders are to be reintegrated.

In this paper I will talk about two Federal Model Projects of exemplary work in de-radicalisation carried through by two NGOs in Berlin – who are at the forefront of such a society conscious approach. One, *Cultures Interactive* (CI), is engaged in communities and schools. Its target group is at-risk adolescents from disadvantaged communities, who are likely to get entangled into extremism, youth delinquency and violence. As its name already indicates, *Cultures Interactive* works with youth-cultures as Hip-Hop, Techno, Gothic etc. But most interesting is, how this is combined with particular pedagogic exercises. The other NGO, *Violence Prevention Network* (VPN), works in prisons and delivers a special group-dynamic training program for young offenders convicted of hate crime, which also includes a systematic approach to civic education.

In the second section of this paper I will refer to two EU research projects, which study these NGOs' quite successful work. The 'good-practice' research aims to find out more about just what it is that makes this work so effectual. One project – "Towards Preventing Violent Radicalisation" (TPVR) – is driven by the London Probation Trust and in Germany focuses on VPN, the second – "Literary and Media Interaction as Means of Understanding and Preventing Adolescent Violence and Extremism" (LIPAV) – is commissioned by the EU's Research Directorate (in the section of psychology/ culture research) and conducted by *Cultures Interactive*. These results will then enable us (1) to draw conclusions as to the criteria for good-practice, inducing pro-social change with the participants and (2) formulate the impact factors of and practice-guidelines for successful de-radicalisation work.

Before I go ahead and give you summaries of these two approaches of intervention, I would like to underline why I have turned to the AIF and proposed this topic: I am convinced, that there are other and comparable pockets of innovation in working with hate crime offenders throughout Europe – and that such initiatives should form a European network and work together more closely. For, it has been found that community organizations and social entrepreneurs in non-profit NGOs – like VPN or CI – can be essential in preventing polarization and violence and intervening into endangered sectors of social life. Often they have been found to be more effective than statutory organizations like criminal justice, probation or state social work. For, other than government employees, NGO-practitioners find it easier to access even the most vulnerable environments and penetrate the language, habit and cultural narratives of (ex-)offenders and their followers.

Therefore, as to de-radicalisation, the European Union Council's 'Stockholm Program – for an open and secure Europe' (2009) stresses: "Key to our success will be the degree to which non-governmental groups ... across Europe play an active part". However, such groups and NGOs' do need professionalization, adhere to quality standards, grant methodological transparency, receive academic and consultancy support, and have (inter-) national exchange of good-practice – which will also provide them with a more stable and productive relationship with governmental bodies at home. Thus, such European network would be helpful in systematically preserving the rich knowledge, skills and services of these non-governmental NGOs and in further developing and mainstreaming their methods into ongoing work.

(I) Two exemplary good-practice approaches of de-radicalisation

What is these two NGOs approach like? How is it exemplary? And what can we learn from them? *Cultures Interactive* (CI) mostly works in East-German communities and increasingly also in inner city districts, be this predominantly "nationalist" or predominantly "ethnic" communities. On occasion CI has also worked with adolescents in Poland and the Czech Republic. The approach of CI combines elements of three kinds:

(a) In their preventive work in disadvantaged communities, the *Cultures Interactive* team brings in young representatives from urban youth-cultures, who give workshops in youth-cultural activities, as Breakdance, Skateboarding, Slam Poetry/ Rap, Techno-DJ-ing and Digital Music Production as well as Visual Design as in Graffiti or Cartoons/ Comics. This first of all has an important motivational impact, which is crucial, since here one is dealing with adolescents who are hardly accessible any more to school education, because they simply have stopped attending school – and get increasingly cynical about life in western societies in general. Therefore, youth-cultures provide a pathway to reach those, who are already almost un-reachable.

Another quite concrete impact factor is, that in socially deprived communities, the adolescents do not have access to any youth-cultural identification other than being 'national' and 'anti-foreigner' or being 'ethnic' and 'Muslim' respectively. Because: either there weren't any other youth-cultures to begin with, or the two or three left over hip-hoppers of a small town may have been roughed up and driven underground. Delivering first-hand experience in urban youth-cultural practices, therefore, means introducing an element of lived diversity into the community.

Moreover, not only are the instructors authentic representatives of their particular youth-culture, they give their workshops in a historically conscious and pedagogical apt fashion.

Firstly, while guiding the exercise of youth-cultural techniques, the instructors also teach about the civil rights background and the situations of dreadful social plight, that these youth-cultures generally come from. Hardly anybody in these courses – and also the school teachers of the young people – are aware of the fact, that HipHop came from deprived neighbourhoods in US American inner city ghettos, which are stricken by violence, drug-traffic, gang-related crime, sexism, racism, and homophobia. Hardly anybody is aware that it is for this very reason, that HipHop has developed an ethos of anti-violence, of life without drugs and of respect for everybody.

Secondly, the instructors are prepared to confront and discuss those aspects of the contemporary HipHop-industry, which mystify violence and sexism as for instance gangster rap or porn rap. Thus, youth-cultures are not only motivating, they also contain many opportunities to raise issues, which are essential both for de-radicalisation, and for education as such.

(b) This strain of activity is then picked up by the second element of the *Cultures Interactive* approach: civic education, which means information, instruction and discussion about issues of extremism, NeoNazi organisations, the Third Reich, xenophobia and the like, – and also about what the benefits of human rights and of living in a free society are. This second element of the CI approach encompasses pedagogical exercises and role plays, which aim at conveying social and emotional skills to the participants as for instance: emotional self-control, non-aggressive conflict solution, the capacity to debate and moderate different opinions.

Furthermore, post-classical civic education, as *Cultures Interactive* practices it, also includes a particular approach of "narrative" interaction, in which stories are told, and the personal living environment is focused. "Narrative" interaction, in a word, means: If you talk to an at-risk young person or even an imprisoned hate crime offender, and if you want her or him to change the behaviour, you better do without leveling arguments and referring to ethical principles, as classical civic education might do. Much more powerful it will be, to have the individual tell her or his stories, and engage in what these stories tell you about the personal experiences and subjective angel, because then you can really work with the person and are not restricted to difficult and always debatable task of discussing arguments and rectifying ideological stance.

(c) Having made very good experiences with this post-classical form of narrative civic education, *Cultures Interactive* went even further and included some elements which are normally found in psycho-therapy. Because telling stories is a quite personal process, a group setting of free talk was introduced, which basically functions as a self-awareness group. It is labeled the "We-Amongst-Ourselves-Group", and it has proven tremendously effective in getting in touch with the teenagers, forging a personal connection and having them open up to each other and the facilitator, in the sense, that they also become more able to take something in, meaning: to see things somewhat different than before. It has been amazing, how much the quality of the workshops in youth-cultures and civic education was raised, since this self-awareness group was introduced.

This leads us directly to *Violence Prevention Network*. This NGO has developed special training for those juveniles in prison, who are convicted of violent crimes and Hate Crimes, imbedded in a Neo-Nazi or Islamist context. And this training is a group-training, working on what has happened in the past, and dealing with one's self in the present – and above all within the training group. A crucial prerequisite to take part is the person's willingness to speak to a group about oneself, about ones lives prior to prison, about families and friends, ones political orientations – and in particular about the acts of violence one has committed. This distinguishes the *Violence Prevention Network* program from classical methods such as anti-aggression training. In this approach, the young adults are not reduced to their being a criminal offender. Instead, each one is taken seriously and is respected as a person, who has his own strengths and weaknesses, and his own history. At the same time, however, the offender will eventually be confronted – before the group and with the help of the group. He is prompted to take responsibility for what he did and arrange for a violence-free future life. So, the approach is an accepting and understanding one, and it is a confrontational approach at the same time, since the person is accepted, but not the crime – which is confronted.

Just as with *Cultures Interactive*, the first group sessions focus on life histories. The individuals are encouraged to explore their memories of humiliation, and their own experiences with violence and abandonment – experiences, which they themselves often do not have much of an emotional response to. They then recognize the connections with their readiness to use violence and adopt attitudes which are politically or religiously extremist.

At the same time a feeling of trust, mutual acceptance, and a willingness to help each other, is developed in the group. Methods like pedagogical exercises, roll playing, drawing a biography curve, assist the process. This confidence is needed for the violence sessions, which are the central element of the group work – and which every participant has agreed to take part in. These violence sessions aim at reconstructing the actions and feelings during the violent act itself. They are highly demanding for trainers and the group alike. Curiously, confronting the inhuman brutality and the ghastly injuries, inflicted on the victims often proves as being just too much for the offenders themselves. But they quite aptly assist each other, without letting anyone of the hook. After this strenuous group experience, most of the individuals are able to accept their responsibility and build a new sense of self and of empathy with others.

Practical exercises in dealing with situations of conflict, provocation and insult, without resorting to violence, complement the program, as well as family and friends sessions in the prison, and a post-release coaching.

Working with the participants' right-wing or fundamentalist attitudes is an undeviating and challenging task throughout the training. However, going through a group process of this kind makes this task decidedly more feasible.

The main target of this work is public protection, i.e. that the rate of re-offending, which with hate crime is generally estimated at around 80% is reduced – and thus the number of victims is reduced.

(II) Two EU projects of empirical good-practice research

Due to the limited space, the findings of these two separate studies which have recently been undertaken on the projects[1], will be synthesized to what is there common denominator. What exactly is it that makes these two quite comparable approaches – the one in prisons, the other in community prevention work – so effective? For, while both NGOs clearly demonstrated good practice in working with vulnerable youths in the field of Hate Crime, the precise factors and conditions behind their effectiveness have yet to be explained. Hence, both studies had to first answer the question of *how and according to which criteria* good-practice may be recognized. Also, besides the

---

[1]   ,Towards Preventing Violent Radicalisation' (TPVR, EU-Directorate ,Justice'); 'Literary and Media Interaction as Means of Understanding and Preventing Adolescent Violence and Extremism'' (LIPAV, Marie-Curie-Program, Directorate Research).

quantitative criterion of a significant reduction in the recidivism or offending rate, the research needed to pinpoint qualitative indicators in order to be able to make good-practice discernible on the spot, to systematically develop further the method, and to make it transferable to different countries and cultural contexts. For, only then is good-practice transferable, if one is able to go beyond describing its methodical elements, which mostly are quite evident, but if one also knows the intervention's less visible *impact factors*.

Therefore this research …

1. … inductively reconstructs how the offenders' and vulnerable persons' 'processes of developmental change' work during the intervention and also explain why the change processes work the way they do, and, following from this, determine which impact factors are at work and which criteria are most helpful and reliable in assessing these change processes.
2. … and provides general, transferable recommendations for the methodology of de-radicalisation work which apply to various cultural contexts and national milieus of social work in prison and in probation.

Methodologically, in both projects a qualitative-empirical design was used that makes use of open, non-thematic methods as biographical-narrative and focused-narrative interviews with participants and facilitators, group discussions and participative observation. Data pertaining to research questions regarding the *factor of culture* – on other words: asking how the individuals of such target groups draw on and makes use of cultural/fictional narratives from film, TV, song lyrics, etc. (which pertains mostly to the LIPAV project) – was collected using a specific media-experience interview and in part via a group-analytical media interview. This sub-field of the research investigates the question how and to what degree of success the person, in his or her mental treatment of a fictional narrative selected by him or herself, consistently attempts or avoids to confront a particular personal "developmental challenge" that possibly also has to do with his or her delinquency or vulnerability to delinquency. This material likewise was evaluated using a sequence-analytical, abductive hypothesis-forming technique, which in addition to the usual analytical steps also draws on the resources of clinical psychology and psychotherapeutic research.

What then has been found in these two studies to be the empirically most reliable indicators of an ex-offender's or vulnerable person's enduring pro-social change?

(A)Appreciation for personal memories: Here the studies came to a counter-intuitive answer: One might intuitively expect that criteria like 'offender's remorse', 'their insight in the condemnable and destructive nature of his actions and attitude', or 'their empathy for the victim' are useful criteria for assessing successful de-radicalisation. The two studies however show that one of the most unfailing and comprehensive indicators of mental change processes is that the offender/ vulnerable person shows a new attitude about and *appreciation for personal memories* and for the *emotional experience of remembering*, irrespective of the subject matter of the memory; and that the person has, thus, increased his/her capacity to uncover, bring to mind, emotionally re-experience, and also verbalize memories of personally lived-through events. In light of this, it has been assessed as particularly indicative if 'memories with a *positive emotional charge*' are expressed/valorized and also if such memories pertain directly to what the person experienced during the intervention when working with the group.

The two studies document and analyse various pieces of interview material supporting the above hypotheses and draw upon empirical violence studies research to further explain why it is, that successful de-radicalisation is indicated by the person's 'appreciation for personal and emotionally positive memories' or simply speaking, by the offenders' or vulnerable persons' getting in touch with what they experienced during their life history – and in her/his experience during the pedagogical intervention spent with the group.

In particular the studies show the wide *scope of indicators* pointing towards the impact factor 'appreciation for personal memories', ranging from quite evident to less visible clues. The range spans from (rare) emphatic expressions such as "this was the first time in my life, I had such a memory ... that I created a memory like that ... and this memory is still in my head, to this day ..." to less discernible indicators such as "this is awful ... I can't remember anything we said [in the training] ... but I'd love to, because the training was great fun mostly ... I'd love to tell you more ... and then we could write a book about it". This tends to be the case in people who suffer from Attention Deficit Disorder with very little access to and verbalization capacity for memories about personally lived emotional experience, who, however, may at least have discovered a strong personal wish to remember more.

Isolating the criterion of 'memory/ emotional recall' is not to say, that observations pertaining to the offender's remorse; their insight in the condemnable nature of his behaviour; or their empathy for the victim may not be significant guidelines of reconstruction. It just means that the new *appreciation for personal memories* and for the *emotional experience of remembering* is more reliable and indicative as an analytical criterion for enduring personal change. In an interview or during intervention, the expression of empathy or remorse may sometimes be the result of pretence, self-deception or simply of good-will which, however, might then all the more easily break down in the face of real-life conditions. Furthermore, such seemingly obvious criteria will keep us from discerning less obvious and more important change-processes and they do not give us any help when facing interview material in which no expression of empathy or remorse can be found.

(B)Personal confidence and trust: A second essential indicator which witnesses mental change processes of de-radicalisation is that the offender/ vulnerable person shows signs that *he/she has built personal confidence and trust* with facilitators and with the group; and that the person has thus, increased their capacity to built trust in relationships and stay trustful even over quite challenging, conflicting, and exhausting experiences of (group) interaction. Here, the studies document and analyze various passages of interview material which show how indicators of trust-building look like with these target groups of individuals. Reference to empirical violence research underlines how significant – and indicative – issues of trust are with these individuals, who tend to not trust anyone easily and sometimes lean towards almost paranoid modes of perception and interaction.

(C)Narrative interaction: As third essential indicator for processes of mental change and de-radicalisation it has been reconstructed: The offender/ vulnerable person shows a new sense and appreciation for *telling stories*/ narrating personally experienced occurrences and actively listen to such narrations; and the person has, thus, increased his/her capacity to *partake in narrative interaction'*. This criterion, which is likely to coincide with the criteria of 'memory' and 'trust', may take into consideration any given narrative, irrespective of its content. However, it particularly pays attention to the narratives which the person gives about conflict-ridden and affectively charged subject matters – as is touched upon for instance while working on the offender's biography, and on his biographical history of violence and denigration/ humiliation, as well as in the reconstruction of the violent crime scene (particularly in the VPN courses).

The two studies proceed to document and analyze interview material which shows different aspects of „appreciation for and capacity of *narrating* personally experienced occurrences", as well as of different qualities of *personal story-telling* in terms of coherence, completion, and emotional saturation. Furthermore, in reference to narratological research the studies underline the importance of 'narrative listening' and 'co-narrative interaction' as well as the necessity that the method of intervention provides story-generating tools.

(D)Emotional learning: As a further essential indicator for mental processes of de-radicalisation it has been determined: „that the offender/ vulnerable person shows signs which indicate experiences of *'emotional learning/emotional intelligence building'*, i.e. that the person shows signs that /s/he begins to realize and reflect upon her/ his own affects and upon situations in which s/he was mostly guided by emotions. This might include observations and thoughts about what consequences these emotions had and maybe even: how the situation could have had a different outcome and how one could possibly take influence on and moderate ones emotions in comparable scenes of interaction (which one module of both approaches systematically picks up on by role-play training of emotional scenes). Here the studies analyze the pertinent interview material as to what the contexts and setting conditions are under which such experiences of 'emotional learning' may occur and further develop.

Particular attention is paid to indications which signal build-up of emotional memory and emotional learning around scenes/ emotions of *embarrassment/ shame, insecurity, fear*, and *helplessness* – be it helplessness in the actual group of the intervention and/or in prior life situations, since scenes with such emotional charge are most remote from verbalization and self-reflection and often linked to dynamics of escalating aggression. Also this indicator is likely to be relevant in situations in which issues of *political convictions*, partisanship, and extremism as well as issues of *religious believe*, feelings, and fundamentalism play a role.

(E)Dealing with ambivalence: A further indicator, which is often closely linked to the above mentioned scenes, pertains to issues of ambivalence and of dealing with ambivalence, or, one step before this, concerns interview passages in which the person recognizes others and/or oneself as being contentious in nature, i.e. as being of two or more minds about concrete real-life situations and about other people and of having to make decisions and negotiate compromise. This indicator is, about leaving behind the 'black and white' world and entering in a world of different shades of color.

(F)Capacity to argue: As further indicator for mental processes of de-radicalisation was found to be that the person shows signs of a newly build appreciation for and *capacity to argue or struggle with others in non-destructive ways* - be it issues of political, religious, or personal nature, i.e. to argue without either turning abusive/ verbally violent or withdrawing and cutting off the interaction. Particularly indicative are signs of a newly built capacity to interact and negotiate conflict *in group situations* – which generally increases the level of fear/aggression and tend to be more regressive in their affective dynamic than interactions between two or three persons.

(3)The impact factors in good-practice de-radicalisation work

One of the most significant factors in the impact of *Violence Prevention Network's* (VPN) social-therapeutic group-work techniques as well as of *Cultures Interactive's* (CI) approach of youth cultural social training has proved to be, that the interventions were able to generate an interactive atmosphere in which a trusting and resilient relationship was established both towards the facilitators as well as within the group itself. This "trust" proved to be essential, as an all-or-nothing condition, without which the pedagogic techniques and methodical exercises would only have been of limited impact and barely capable of prompting a lasting change in the individual's attitude and behaviour.

Why this should have been the case was not immediately obvious. Nevertheless, it was already known from empirical violence research that people tending towards violent and extreme behaviour live according to a marked system of distrust that can sometimes assume paranoid features.[2] The question, however, as to how, in psychody-

---

[2]   On the „paranoid style of attribution" in „violent imprisoned men" as well as the tendency towards

namic terms, this mistrust is conditioned and obtained, and above all how VPN's and CI's intervention method still managed to generate trust and resilience, remained for large parts of the research unanswered.

Initially it was possible to isolate a few formal factors:

1) it seemed to be of utmost importance that the facilitators *come from outside* and not from within the environment of the institution itself. Obviously, the prison is particularly susceptible to distrust. It is very difficult for a prison psychologist to succeed in credibly guaranteeing the confidentiality of the conversation when he or she has a direct institutional involvement in decisions that are life-altering for the prisoner. However in any youth-work contexts of violence prevention, it generally also proves quite recommendable that the team be independent from the everyday contexts of the young people. Above all the components of the self-awareness-group required a protected space that internal staff and facilitators would have been unable to provide.

2) That is by no means to say, however, that the institutional environment should remain uninvolved, or that it should not accept and absorb the external impulse, and support and extend it using the means available to it. On the contrary – and this is the second formal factor: the effectiveness of the two approaches (VPN and CI) was closely connected to the necessity of involving in the intervention's sphere of impact not only the young people themselves, but also and in principle the *institutions and local environments* to which they belong. It is therefore propitious and helpful when these institutions expressly signal their "respect" for these "outsiders", for example by simultaneously commissioning training for staff members and by seeking institutional consultancy. *Violence Prevention Network* therefore also often works with prison employees and takes on consultancy roles in higher-level administrative-technical and political structures. *Cultures Interactive* offers vocaltiona trainings to social workers and school teachers. This consultancy activity gave rise to networking effects that in turn had a positive effect on the work with the young people themselves.

3) The third formal factor contributing significantly to the generation of trust and re-silience, and thus to the lasting impulses for change that arose, is the fact that VPN's and CI's work is done *in the group and with the group*. The research interviews clearly indicate that the basic trust of the participants, and thus the degree of impact that the behaviour-altering effects have upon them, are crucially dependent upon a *group-dynamic* approach being taken. In other words, it is essential that attention is paid to the *processes* and the *developments* of the participants in the group and their *relation-ships* towards each another, and that these processes and relations are conceived of as the primary object of the group work. It is clear that what is said and experienced by

„preventative attack", cf. Tedeschi, J.T. (2002): Die Sozialpsychologie von Aggression und Gewalt. In Heitmeyer/ Hagan: Internationales Handbuch der Gewaltforschung, Westdeutscher Verlag. p. 585.

attentive and active participants in a professionally-led group goes much deeper and has a doubly lasting impact.

This observation seems to be particularly pertinent with the groups of young people at issue here, because almost all violent hate-crimes are generated by clique behaviour – and thus are the product of uncontrolled processes of a so-called escalating *anti-group dynamic*.[3] It is therefore all the more true to say that in both approaches an essential social-therapeutic goal of the work is the ability to enter into, maintain and make use of triangular (at the minimum), multi-pronged and complex group relationships. These methods of intervention therefore intuitively placed emphasis on demanding from their participants the art of talking openly and personally within the group, and of being confidential and discreet outside the group – without at the same time insisting that they be utterly silent and act as though they were members of a secret society.

Moreover, the ability to successfully practice trust, confidentiality and "respect" across the range of loyalties and group- and relationship-contexts in one's life and school/ work environment can be seen as the highest goal of *civic education*, in the post-classical sense of anti-bias work. After all, societies in which the opposite of freedom, liberality and non-violence predominate can be recognized simply enough by the absence in them of trust and confidentiality, and instead the presence of indiscretion/de-nunciation, intrigue, surveillance, fear/exercise of power, and selfish segregation – a misanthropic and anti-social situation that can exist in smaller or larger groups and for which terms such as "anti-democratic" or "extremist" are far too vague. It seems all the more appropriate, then, to aim for what can only be achieved through dynamic and open group-work, namely to provide participants with the ability to find their way in a world consisting of occasionally conflicting and competing groups, and to provide them with the necessary abilities of self-integration and self-delineation.

More broadly, the findings also point to the fact that *the one-to-one supervisor*, no matter how talented, is unable to through his or her work to achieve this demanding pedagogic goal, and that the expectations and self-images of practitioners often equate to a systematic (self-)over-exertion that negatively affect the work. This is especially true for the target group in question here, since violent offenders, or those vulnerable to such behaviour, often grew up fatherless (because the latter were absent either de facto or emotionally). They were thus socialized in a dyadic and *tendentially symbiotic two-way relationship*, which was mostly cramped, insufficiently delineated and chronically over-exerted. For this reason, all social- or psychotherapeutic interven-

---

[3]   On the other hand, it should be said that the psychopathic individual offender fundamentally requires forensic psychiatry and is out of place in normal prison and its capacity for intervention. It is particularly important to point this out given the misleading question occasionally expressed as to whether it does not constitute a limitation of a technique such as VPN that it only applies to a selected sub-group of violent offenders. It became evident that the technique, as soon as the necessary framework conditions are provided, can in principle be applied to all types and all degrees of crime. (And even in forensics, excellent work is done with – psychotherapeutic – groups.)

tions carried out between two persons are subordinated to additional structural limits that, in the interest of quality assurance, should be cause for concern. Having said that, the two- or three-way conversation has an important *supplementary function* (especially in prison work) and is above all useful when individual results need to be consolidated or when individuals have to be stabilized because the group process becomes too intense for them – a permanent risk with precariously situated groups such as this. Accordingly, the results also indicated that a further formal factor influencing trust-building lies in the precise *dosage of group intensity*, which is regulated through flexible setting changes from the whole group to small groups and to two-way conversations, or through the change to pedagogic exercises and role plays. Nevertheless, it appears to be crucial to the success of the work that *the group* always remains the main point of reference, against which the various individual measures are placed in perspective.

Above and beyond the formal factors, the interview material also raised connected questions as to how the *professional persona and group-interaction style* of the facilitator contributed to producing the aforementioned prerequisites for generating a climate of "trust and resilience", and how the facilitator succeeded in moderating the interaction within the group in such a way as to be effective in terms of trust and hence of changing behaviour. There are many indications to suggest that the personal attitude of the facilitator represented a *direct influencing factor* – although such observations run the risk of being mystified as a personal talent, whereas in fact it is of a thoroughly technical nature and as such can be communicated and acquired.

Analyzing VPN's and CI's methods revealed a central aspect of this personal facilitation style to be a kind of conversational and group guidance, which can be called the *"lifeworld"* mode or briefly: the *narrative* mode of interaction. This denotes that the centre of the group's attention is occupied by each participant and his or her self and personal experiences, and that the primary interest is the individual, lifeworld experiences of that particular person, to which the other group members relate at an equally personal level. Compared to this, all other components – teaching and training plans, exercises and definite pedagogic content – are assigned a secondary valence, because in order to be lastingly effective they depend on the existence of a relational basis that always offers the possibility for participants to confidently return to narrating their experiences.

In work with violent offenders, then, all morality and all judgments are initially dispensed with. Similarly, in local prevention work, where the primary concern is civil-societal issues of tolerance and diversity, or political educational issues of prejudices and group-directed misanthropy, then any argumentation, information and ethical or value-based considerations are initially put to one side. In both cases, the working approach is primarily concerned with the release of the individual, lifeworld narratives of the participants; with their *subjective experiential perspectives* and *biographical early histories* – and with the exchange of these perspectives with the other members of the group. In this respect, the two approaches intuitively followed the *pedagogical primacy of narration*, and it discovered and took to heart the fact that people, especially when it comes to making lasting changes to their attitude and behaviour, open up when they are able to *develop their personal narration in a trusting relationship*, to do so in a way that reveals areas of their individual experience, and when they can share these perspectives with other people in a process of group exchange. Aspects of ethics, morality and judgment then seem to return of their own accord, not from the facilitators, but rather from personal motivation.

Of course, the experienced practitioner will hardly be surprised by this. It is well known that morality, judgment, arguments and information have always demonstrated limited effects; people have been quite right to warn against "overestimating" the "power of factual arguments" as opposed to the level of "feelings and emotions"[4]). This is truest of all for vulnerable youths, who automatically react with cynical contempt or inner retreat wherever moral or pedagogic value pressure is generated. Yet regardless of how well known this fact is, it often seems difficult to abandon the moral-judgmental impetus and to acquire and to put into practice a *facilitator style of lifeworld-narrative and relationship-based access*. This, at any rate, represented a particular challenge both for VPN and CI when it came to training new co-workers and introducing them to the work and the *facilitation style* of the approach – which was after all an innovative, self-developed approach.[5]

In concrete terms, the difficulty for methodological approaches like this consists primarily in motivating participants to even begin with *trusting narration* – given that as a rule they are often somewhat disinclined to talk about themselves and about emotional subjects. The ability to narrate in this sense of the term is a quite difficult skill that requires the person first recognizes their own subjective narrative perspective as such, and that he or she is sufficiently familiar with its content in order then to be able to present narrative episodes as detailed and accessible stories and to exchange these stories with others. However the greatest objective difficulty is above all the fact that the personal experiences recalled by this group of participants, for example in the area familial background, often involve exceedingly negative experiences that can only with considerable difficulty (or not at all) be narrated spontaneously – and as such, block other more immediate narrative content.

The skill of narrating is also difficult insofar as the narration – and this is especially the case with negative subject matters – can take a form that is always more or less *detailed and conducive to personal development*. As is well-known, one can "lie to

---

4   Cf. Spangenberg, R.: http://www.politische-bildung-brandenburg.de/extrem/praevention.html

5   However it became all the more clear how necessary it is to continue, by means of systematic accompanying research, objectifying, documenting and didacticising good practice techniques, in order to provide orientation for further methodological developments in this and other areas of social work and „education".

oneself", "kid" oneself and others, remember essential details "only dimly" and joint-ly cultivate anti-narrational defense mechanisms. On the other hand, together with the group, one can take risks in narrational self-discovery – which in principle produces social-therapeutic effects. From a narratological perspective, it should be recalled that psychotherapy as such is defined allegorically as the "continual re-telling of one and the same story", only that this one story "is re-told ever better" (Roy Schafer). This can be taken to mean that, through narrative representation, the decisive episodes of a person's biography and life-world can 1) be increasingly elaborated and completed, so that 2) they can gain increasing intensity in emotional expression and in the affective engagement of the narrator. Thereby the emotionality of the narration increasingly comes to approximate what was thought and felt during the experience itself.

This *process of narrative-forming* often extends to the listeners and co-narrators in the group, and/or is to a great extent prompted and supported by them.[6] The "better" – in a narratological sense – the story is told, the greater the probability of releasing long-lasting impulses for personal change and development. From a scientific perspective, too, there is a great deal to be said for trying to elicit development-conducive forms of narrative in the group, and for that reason for the facilitator to adopt the attitude of *lifeworld-narrative and relationship-based access* as the benchmark for the group-culture being aimed for in the intervention.

In view of the quite wide spread programs of fully modularized *cognitive-behavioral trainings* in various areas of socio-therapeutic and social work, it can be said that it is this very element of *lifeworld-narrative and relationship-based* interaction and *co-narrative* dynamic – often called also open-process interaction – which is missing there. Experienced practitioners in this field share the impression that the avoidance of narrative, open-process interaction goes back to a institutional and/or personal hes-itation or inability to build trust and relationship with violent offenders and vulnerable persons and that this, for a fair number of these trainings, is the main reason of their relatively limited success in bringing about lasting effects.

How, then, did the facilitators proceed in order to initiate a *narrative process quality* of this sort?

Throughout it was possible to observe that the group and workshop facilitators in their own ways signaled *their personal readiness to enter a relationship*. In doing so, they made use in particular of the basic fact that the more one demonstrates a credible per-sonal interest and a *"reliable attentiveness"*, the more open others are, both towards themselves and in the way they speak about themselves. However this attentiveness has

---

6   The biography researcher Gabriele Rosenthal has in this connection spoken of narrated and experienced life stories. In: (1995). Erzählte und erlebte Lebensgeschichte. Gestalt und Struktur biographischer Selbstbeschreibungen. Frankfurt a.M. (Campus). Rosenthal, G. (2004). Biographical Research. In: Seale, C., Gobo, G., Gubrium, J.F. & Silverman, D. (Eds.). Qualitative Research Practice. London: Sage, 48-64.

to be entirely credible and to stand up to all kinds of testing – especially with young people, who relentlessly and minutely scrutinize their counterparts before they trust them.

As concerns the central question as to which further conditions need to be fulfilled so that this trustworthiness and attentiveness at the level of the personal relationship can be reliably applied, the evaluation resulted above all in two findings. Helpful, though as a rule overestimated, is the ability and the readiness of the facilitator to involve *themselves as a person* and sometimes also to reveal personal information about themselves, in order to appear to others as authentic and inspire trust. However this factor is in fact demanded by young people lesser than is generally thought – and sometimes feared. In most cases, the questioning from the adolescents is a matter of fairly uncomplicated and easily manageable initiatives in order to carry out a first contact probe, something that basically is very welcome. (Notably, in almost all cases the facilitators tended to respond to the questions directly and in a measured fashion, without insisting too soon on professional abstinence and neutrality, which comes into play at a later stage during more critical moments. The facilitators, with their process- and relation-oriented approach, go on the basis that a principled abstinence would – logically enough – be understood by the young people to mean that there is something else, something external, that is more important to the facilitator than the working relationship at hand, and that therefore that the young person him- or herself is of merely secondary importance).

On the other hand, what is generally underestimated, despite it being of central importance, is that the openness and the attentiveness of the facilitator, though thematically unrestricted, is by no means entirely unconditional. Successful praxis was characterized by the fact that the facilitator demonstrates an attitude that can be called an *attitude of critical attentiveness*. Essential for this is that the facilitator, alongside his or her credible guarantee of confidentiality and trustworthiness, also unreservedly expresses any (un)reasonable doubts, conjectures or enquiries concerning the statements, representations and stories of the participants, and that an atmosphere is thereby created in which everyone can show their true colours and thus, by daring to express themselves, enter into negotiations over their relationships. This is standard in dynamically-open group work, however by and large something that the young people barely have experience of.

Critical attentiveness, in other words, deals with precisely this conflict-prone contact and the frictional points of reference, without of course acting in a way that is aggressive or deprecatory, or even overbearing or suggestive. It is far more the case that the facilitators pursued the goal of practicing an exemplary mode of *respectful skepticism*, which does not jeopardize the dignity of the person, but which, on the contrary, for the first time gives the person's dignity its due. (While "human dignity" is only very formally guaranteed by an undifferentiated and contact-abstinent notion of tolerance or acceptance, in a successful negotiation of difference it can be properly given credit.)

The *critical attentiveness* practiced by theses two approaches observes the basic difference between person and criminal offence, and thus corresponds to a fundamental attitude that is *as accepting as it is confrontational*.[7] One might have thought that this combination would be impossible (at least if one bases one's assumptions on the discourse of classical political education or youth work), however it has proved essential as a technique of intervention.

Moreover, this combination contains a specific pedagogical value. The *attitude of critical attentiveness* involves the practice of a skill that this target group can be seen to be sorely lacking, yet one they urgently need to learn: the ability to get along with people who are very "different", to overcome large subjective perceptions of difference, and to act acceptingly-attentively as well as, in critical moments, critically-confrontationally. They must also learn to maintain this ability in emotionally dynamic group situations – and not to react, as they had previously, with avoidance, uncompromising schism or violent escalation.

Particularly as concerns the "lifeworld-narrative" technique, the *"culture factor"* opens up a highly original spectrum of methodological possibilities – that are not yet systematically used by *Violence Prevention Network*, but showed their potential with the work of *Cultures Interactive*. The trusting narration of personal experience can be particularly effectively prompted and intensified using cultural and fictional narrative and/or individual creativity. Particularly with youths from problem areas, a group which is hard to reach, *Cultures Interactive* employs forms of praxis taken from urban youth culture that offer the young adults readily accessible methods for personal self-expression, and which can thereby help to attain a significant deepening of the pedagogic process. Even drawing on films or song texts that the participants indicate to be personally important or interesting, opens up numerous possibilities for working on biographical or lifeworld experiences, which can then be taken up in the group discussion. In a person's mental handling of a fictional narrative of his or her own choice, particular personal themes or "developmental challenges" are consistently brought to the fore that can be used for the shared process. Of course the prerequisite for this is that a *lifeworld-narrative and relationship-based access* approach is used and that the facilitator practices an *attentive-critical attitude*.

In comparison with the fundamentally different, what could be called behaviouristic approaches, it can be said that, when taken out of context, individual elements out of a complex technique like the VPN or CI approach have proven barely to function and sometimes even to be unadvisable – in other words, to remove particular exercises, role plays, methods of arrangement or didactic modules of civic education from the

---

[7]   Also cf. Harris, D.M., Selyn, J. & Bush J.: Positive and Supportive Authority: An Approach to Offender Management and Supervision (in preparation), and: Harris, D.M. & Riddy, R. (2008). The Thinking Skills Programme Facilitation Manual. Ministry of Justice. Harris, D.M. & Bush, J. (2010). Ono to One Cognitive Self Change. NOMS Cymru.

concept as a whole, and to practice them outside the trusting, process-based and relational context of the directed group, will barely be successful. Even maintaining the process-based context requires that care must be taken not to carry out the modules, exercises and role-plays etc. too early, before the framework of trust necessary for life-world narrative work has been reliably generated. This is because there is a danger that the exercises are only performed by the participants for the sake of politeness, or that they descend into more or less open boredom, and that the biographical investigations remain superficial and clichéd.

The even greater risk of a technique that tries to employ selected exercises while dispensing with the context of relations, process and group, is that in acutely emotional situations particularly vulnerable individuals will enter states of fear and rage, since they are unable to rely on the security of a relational framework of trust, one that because of their psychologically fragile condition they absolutely require. Methods such as the "hot seat", where the violent offender is provoked with insults and physical assault, so that he learns not to lose control and resort to violence, need to be cautioned against. People that have learned both the narrative and the pure training approache were able to provide particularly useful assessments here. External assessments also reached the conclusion that methodically isolated provocation exercises of this sort are disadvantageous. They run the danger of exacerbating precisely what these young people can do all too well (and what is not good for them): bottling things up and hanging in there, until in real life the affect breaks out – at the expense of others. A *critical-attentive* attitude and systematic relational and narrative work in the trust-framework of the group is therefore an essential prerequisite if individual exercises and modules are to have a lasting and low-risk impact. It is all the more important to emphasize this, since in the last decade anti-aggression work has been strongly characterized by such approaches.[8]

(4) Summary of impact factors and practice guidelines

Hence, to sum up, the good-practice research on *Violence Prevention Network's* and *Cultures Interactive's* methods of intervention has formulated the following criteria indicating that a method is effective and that participants begin to embark on favorable changes of attitude and behaviour. Valid criteria are any signs which indicate that the offender/ vulnerable person

(1) has begun to build a greater degree of *personal confidence and trust* with facilitators and with the group – and thus increased his capacity to built trust in relationships even during conflicting and challenging phases of (group) interaction.

---

[8]   It is possible to learn a this lesson through a similar methodological trend in psychotherapy: the family arrangement of Bernd Hellinger. Here, the long-established and highly effective methodological element of „family constellation" has been removed from the therapeutic (trust) framework and been used as an isolated – and sensational – technique. The bitter consequence has been psychiatric internments and suicides, as well as occasionally highly questionable ideological implications.

(2) has begun to build a new attitude about and appreciation for *personal memories* and for the emotional experience of *remembering personally lived-through events* – in particular positively charged events.

(3) has begun to developed a new sense and appreciation for *telling stories/* narrating personally experienced occurrences – regardless of what scope and significance the experience has – and actively listen to such narrations, and thus increased his/her capacity to *partake in narrative interaction.*

(4) has made experiences of *emotional learning / building emotional intelligence* and thus has begun to realize and reflect upon one's own personal emotions and about situations of emotional involvement – in particular situations and emotions of embarrassment/ shame, insecurity, fear, and helplessness.

(5) has acquired some recognition of *personal ambivalence* and has thus experienced that he himself and/or others often are of two minds about concrete real-life situations and that one has to make decisions and negotiate compromise.

(6) has begun to built a new appreciation for and capacity *to argue or struggle with others in non-destructive ways* – be it issues of political, religious, or personal nature, i.e. to argue without either turning verbally abusive or withdrawing from the interaction.

In view of these basic criteria of favorable personal changes, the following impact factors and practice-guidelines for de-radicalisation work could be determined: The methodological prerequisites of any successful approach are

(i) that the facilitators of the pedagogic intervention come from *outside the institution* and are able to act independently; this is required in light of the indispensable process of confidence-building which is generally most difficult to achieve with this target group; being able to provide a *secure and confidential space* for the participants to speak and interact, seems to be one of the most important success factors of these approaches;

(ii) that the *institution* does, however, signal its high esteem of the incoming outside facilitators (which requires containment of any impulses of professional competitiveness or feelings of envy) and that the institution itself is *interested and actively involved* – for example in staff training or workshops given by these facilitators;

(iii) above all, that significant parts of the work takes place *in the group and with the group*, and thus attention is paid to the processes and developments in and of the participants and their *group-dynamic* relationships with one another, a prerequisite which is due to the fact that hate crimes are generally group-dynamically induced and that hate crime offenders and vulnerable persons have often been raised in overexerted one-on-one relationships to their single parents – and therefore are all the less experienced in and more vulnerable to escalating group-dynamics;

(iv) that a *conducive dosage* of group intensity (off-set with pedagogical exercises and supplementary-supportive one-on-one conversations) is borne in mind;

(v) that the professional persona and intervention style of the facilitator focuses on generating a *trusting and resilient* relationship, both in the group and in the one-on-one sessions, and that this relationship is nurtured constantly;

(vi) but also, that a facilitator style of *critical attentiveness* is adopted which also seeks out points of contention and conflict, at the same time observing the basic distinction between the person, which is accepted, and the offence, which is confronted – so that an *respectfully-enquiring exchange* can proceed *both acceptingly and confrontationally*;

(vii) that on the basis of this relationship a mode of *lifeworld-narrative* and *relationship-based* access to the young people is created that enables the occurrence of a trusting and *development-conducive* narrative about personal experience;

(viii) that the factor of *civic education*, political and ideological exchange as well as the *factor of culture* is incorporated (for instance in the form of fictional media narratives) in order to add to the experiential depth of the pedagogical process;

(ix) that the intervention on the whole does, however, feel compelled to following an entirely strict syllabus; due to the above stated principle of the *lifeworld-narrative* and *relationship-based* approach, the need for an *open process* is acknowledged in which the participants group's spontaneous issues are given priority;

(x) the principle of working with an open process *lifeworld-narrative* and *relationship-based* approach also implies *methodological flexibility* and *eclecticism* with regard to pedagogic tools and therapeutic resources. In particular, the studies and other topical evaluations have recently demonstrated the pitfalls and deficits of two approaches which have been quite predominate during the last decade: (a) pure *anti-aggression trainings* by themselves as well as (b) fully modularized *cognitive-behavioral trainings* seem to have had less effect then previously assumed – unless they are embedded into and off-set with an open-process narrative framework of proceedings;

(xi) that *protective relationships* are inaugurated already during prison time, calling on suitable family members, friends or community members whose personality is fitting the needs and challenges of reintegrating hate crime offenders/ vulnerable persons;

(xii) that with de-facto offenders in prison a *post-release coaching* is put into place which assists them in beginning their new life in the community.

These conditions seem propitious for setting in motion mental processes that in turn can lead to the development of essential personality competencies and emotional intelligence and to the alteration of certain attitudes and forms of behaviour. Clearly, in the future an innovative, interdisciplinary and application-oriented technique is called for. Also, in the development of such innovative interventional methods for use in social work, there are good reasons to look for possible ways in which both the factor of culture and culture studies and the clinical-therapeutic field might be of assistance – and thus to ease the not always easy relationship between social, cultural and clinical work, and between clinical and cultural/social scientific research.

European Forum for Urban Security (EFUS)

General Assembly – Berlin, 10-11 May 2010

"How cities reconcile security and fundamental rights"

Summary

This year's EFUS General Assembly was hosted by the German Congress on Crime Prevention (GCOCP) – associated member of the Forum - and was part of the 15th edition of this annual event, which brought together almost 4000 experts and practitioners of crime prevention. The EFUS General Assembly had merged with the "Annual International Forum (AIF)" to become this year's international Forum within the Congress.

Opening session: Security and Freedom in a new European and international context

This year again, the effects of globalisation have set the context of the general assembly of the European Forum for Urban Security. Globalisation is far from being a new phenomenon, but the challenges it poses to our policies, our objectives and our methods require a constant adaptation.

In this context, **Erich Marks,** Executive Director of the German Congress on Crime Prevention, presented the labour undertaken at the local level in our cities and the exchanges held over the last period among the different actors, stressing that they need to be strengthened and adapted. More than ever, he said, cities are the place where problems can be most efficiently addressed. Also, he added, cities are directly confronted to the new challenges of globalisation, among others its consequences on our economies and on the environment.

However, the main challenge today is without a doubt the need to reconcile the notions of security and fundamental rights. GCOCP president **Professor Hans-Jürgen Kerner** reminded us that it is indeed a very old debate, and he added that the issues at stake are daunting. In this respect, cities are on the frontline because they are THE place where most people build their lives and evolve personally. The paradox is that safety, which is a fundamental human right, is sometimes used to curb individual freedom. Both safety and freedom can be reconciled if we adopt a positive vision of the city, as the Forum has been doing for years. The Forum's approach is to see the city as a place where everybody can enjoy what we can call a positive safety.

A positive vision of security is inevitably built on a strong preventive approach. As it was clearly shown by **Professor Irvin Waller** from the University of Ottawa, it is undeniable that an ever-more repressive approach does not improve the effectiveness of security policies, without mentioning the fact that it is significantly more expensive than the preventive approach.

The general process of globalisation, evoked by **Erich Marks**, has also led to an important increase in the number of countries having recently adopted an overall crime prevention policy, as shown by the latest report of the International Centre for the Prevention of Crime (ICPC). The ICPC new Director, **Paula Miraglia**, explained that several tools and toolkits had been developed to accompany these countries and provide them with methodological support.

Developing, strengthening and creating preventive actions in developing countries remain a key priority, because these countries register a staggering share of the total of crimes committed worldwide. Most developing countries have undergone a phenomenal urban growth in recent years, with the subsequent collapse of their infrastructures. According to **Alexander Butchart,** of the World Health Organisation (WHO), it is crucial to develop long-term prevention policies and make better use of available funding to allow the citizens of these countries to live in freedom and security. This is also necessary in order to prevent a potential pandemic wave of violence, on a scale never seen.

Round table 1: Ensuring security and fundamental rights in the context of immigrant societies

Living together and sharing the same public space in a non-conflictual way is a daily challenge for European cities, faced with new waves of immigration in the wake of the economic globalisation. What are the causes of conflict?

According to Professor **Harald Weilnböck,** a psychoanalist specialised in inter-cultural relations, the main stream of the societies receiving an important number of immigrants is in fact often not ready to welcome these immigrants. The reasons invoked are multiple: different lifestyles and attitudes towards public spaces, unprepared social services, and a common prejudice against immigrants, who are generally associated with crime. In this context, cities must adopt a pro-active approach and build common grounds for mutual understanding and trust.

An example of this approach was presented by **Francesc Guillén**, from the Generalitat of Catalunya in Spain. He underlined that was first and foremost a social issue and not one of security. There are various ways to ensure a peaceful coexistence (*convivencia* in Spanish), which can be implemented by the cities themselves or with the help of NGOs working together on crime and violence prevention, through groups' dynamics. These actions can be developed in direct contact with the people and should never be based on ideologies (as **Harald Weilnböck** has shown). A balance needs to be found between confrontation and acceptance, between offering specific services to the immigrant population and being firm on the respect of local rules (as argued by **Giorgio Pighi** , Mayor of the city of Modena). Training the municipal staff on diversity and engaging the city in diversity schemes is also the way forward (as shown by **Gilles Nicolas,** Deputy Mayor of the city of Nantes).

The key issue for a peaceful coexistence lies in the dialogue between the various communities who share the public space. This implies:

- identifying key stakeholders,
- sharing views in order to promote understanding and trust,
- working directly with the people, through groups and family dynamics,
- striking a balance between each group's rights and duties,
- promoting the acceptance of diversity, both in terms of recruitment policies and in terms of training, and include this theme in education programmes,
- building common grounds of trust and respect,
- communicating in a responsible manner.

Round Table 2: Security technology supporting fundamental rights?

Today, the use of various security technologies (CCTV, crime mapping, remote alarms, prevention methods on the internet) have created a European-wide debate at the local level. Cities need to find the right balance between answering the citizens' demand for security and guaranteeing the respect of citizens' fundamental rights. Does the right of every citizen to live in a safe area justify the installation of cameras and the use, a posteriori, of the images recorded? In his introduction, **Peter Squires**, Professor at Brighton University, United Kingdom, summed up the debate by asking cities one question: should we use technology to solve our social problems?

Mr Squires explained how CCTV in the UK has been largely oversold. "The effectiveness of this technology is largely questioned today," he said. When we talk of security at city level, CCTV is mainly referred to as a tool for crime prevention, among many other instruments of public safety policies. However, there has been a mission drift from *prevention* to *detection* and today, CCTV can be considered as a tool reserved for the police only. This creates a new risk of seeing the traditional role of the police shifting from serving the community towards managing technology. CCTV surveillance keeps policemen apart from the streets and from the people. Another problem highlighted by Mr Squires comes from the new, so-called intelligent security technology. Indeed, "enhanced" camera systems that "recognise" potentially delinquent behaviours will automatically be focused on certain racial profiles. For instance, a specific way of walking and talking will be recognised as weapon carrying. This drift from the original function can be perceived as a threat to fundamental rights.

The cities invited to share their experiences around the table argued that technology should be incorporated in comprehensive policies. If they are used with balance, they can be useful to:

- respond to citizens' needs in a specific area of the city (the wireless CCTV system in Alcobendas was presented by **Carlos Cremona**),

- deliver, by Youtube or Facebook, prevention messages to groups otherwise hard to reach (presented by **Eija Laihinen** from Helsinski),

- provide specific police assistance to victims of crime (the remote alarm scheme in Liege for shopkeepers and victims of domestic violence was presented by **Sara Debouny** and **Bénédicte Biron**).

The experience of crime mapping realised directly by common citizens with Google maps was also evoked: in this bottom-up approach, public authorities can base their actions on the information provided by the people.

Round Table 3: Involvement of citizens and civil society in crime prevention

Paul Ekblom, Professor of Design against Crime in London (UK), argued that most crime prevention policies are implemented by civilians and individuals, not by professionals. The role of the professional is to support the intervention of the individuals. Frameworks need to be put together in order to include in the extra-judicial system specific civilian crime prevention schemes (in daily life at work, in schools, families, and in the economic and cultural spheres). The crucial question is how to get people involved? This can be done with the collaboration of competent volunteers, provided we define clearly their assignments. Volunteers need to be alerted, informed, empowered (capacity building) and managed. In any case, vigilantism must be avoided.

Sabrina Oesterle, from the University of Washington, Seattle (USA), presented the Communities That Care (CTC) approach in the US and Canada, an approach that also exists in some European countries such as the Netherlands. This approach relies on the creation of community coalitions for effective prevention planning. She explained that with the CTC system, communities are able to use the latest advances in the field of prevention science. She also said that CTC use a public health approach to prevent problematic behaviours among young people, in particular violence, misdemeanours, dropping out of school and substance abuse.

Michela Tassistro, member of the Municipal Council of Genoa (Italy) presented her city's approach to citizens' participation. Security needs to be a dynamic process, she said. Even though security policies are implemented at the national level, under the control of the State, Italian cities play an important role as the voice of local communities. In order to enroll the participation of citizens, certain conditions must be met, argued Ms Tassistro. In particular, the work undertaken by the association of volunteers can complement the actions led by the State. However, she added, the degree of participation of the people depends on how they evaluate the efficiency of the security policies in their own region and cities.

Stephan Voss, director of the Crime Prevention Council of the city-state of Berlin gave an overview of crime prevention in his Land, and presented the organisation in place there. Describing in particular the initiatives taken locally to prevent reoffending, he cited as an interesting example the partnership put in place with organisations of immigrants, in particular Turkish ones. It is very important, he said, to build a platform for dialogue so that issues can be assessed and discussed before actions are undertaken. He said that the fact that organisations of immigrants are on board has lifted a taboo among stakeholders, and created a fruitful debate. He also pointed out that in order to foster citizens' participation in a city as big as Berlin, it is necessary to enroll organisations representing the people, before considering a more direct form of citizens' participation.

Closing session : Local responses in a changing European context for crime prevention - the mission of (D)Efus

The entry into force of the Lisbon Treaty in December 2009 has a considerable impact on security policies. Indeed, several areas that were previously addressed through inter-governmental cooperation are now directly under the competence of the EU. The European Parliament has now more power to decide on a certain number of issues related to security, that will now require a co-decision procedure.

As far as the organisation of the European Commission is concerned, the previous *Justice, Freedom and Security* portfolio has been divided into a security orientated post and a civil rights orientated one. There is now a Commissioner for Home Affairs and a Commissioner for Justice, Fundamental Rights and Citizenship. Another significant development concerns the European Crime Prevention Network (EUCPN), which was reformed a few months ago. A European network promoting crime prevention activity in member States across the EU, the EUCPN is a "meeting point" for governments, researchers and representatives of the civil society. Under the new scheme, it is no longer "piloted" by the European Commission, who previously provided the technical secretariat. Now, member States have more responsibilities since the technical secretariat will be held by one of the national governments, on the basis of a collegial vote. As for the EUCPN secretariat, it is slated to be either complemented or replaced by a European Observatory of Crime Prevention. The Stockholm Programme that defines the European Union's Security policy for 2010-2014 does not include any provision concerning cities specifically, although their role is expanded in the area relative to development projects with Third World countries. As respective action plan is still being discussed at the European Parliament, Efus sees as an opportunity to still make a stand for the importance of the role of local authorities in crime prevention.

The Efus' political stance has recently been reinforced by the creation of a new national Forum, the German Forum for Urban Security or (D)Efus, that will also promote increased cooperation between local and European decision-making bodies.

The seventh national Forum to be part of the Efus, the (D)Efus was officially launched during the general assembly by its newly elected president, Dr Martin Schairer, Deputy Mayor of Stuttgart, and by Erich Marks, Chief Executive of the Lower Saxony Crime Prevention Council and Vice-President of the Efus. The German members of the European forum, which now include the cities of Munich, Mannheim, Düsseldorf, Augsburg, Leer, Heidelberg and Oldenburg as well as the German Congress on Crime Prevention, have created "their" national Forum to foster cooperation on urban security. As the founding members have indicated in the name of the newly created forum, the **German European** Forum for Urban Security - (D)Efus according to its acronym- is both a platform for the German members of the Efus, and also a resolutely European forum acting as a bridge between the European and local instances.

The ten first new German members have immediately agreed to work closer together on prevention issues, and to be more open to and involved with Europe. They also called German cities to join them at both the Efus and (D)Efus.

The creation of the (D)Efus was welcomed by the other members of the Efus and by its newly elected president Guilherme Pinto as a decisive development in the life of the Forum.

Wiebke Steffen

Expert Report

for the 15th German Congress on Crime Prevention
10th & 11th of May 2010 Berlin

"Education – Prevention – Future"
Learning and Living Spaces of Children and Juveniles as Places of Education and Prevention of Violence

0
Summary

The main topic of discussion at the 15th German Congress on Crime Prevention "Education – Prevention – Future" follows up on the problem which had already become apparent in the expert report pertaining to the main discussion topic of the 14th German Congress on Crime Prevention 2009, "Live Solidarity - Secure Diversity". In this congress it became apparent that, at least for Germany, the educational success of the following generations is significantly determined by social class and background. However, education and qualification are the prerequisites for individual opportunities in life and participation in society. Equal opportunities regarding access to education promote integration and participation, and as such also contribute toward the prevention of violence and crime.

The **expert report** on the main topic of the 15th German Congress on Crime Prevention: "Learning and Living Spaces of Children and Juveniles as Places of Education and Prevention of Violence" starts off by taking a look at:

1.

Societal prerequisites and chances which determine education and educational opportunities in Germany and which have particularly detrimental effects on children and juveniles of the lower social groups and those with a migrational background. It goes on to look at the challenges and requirements related to social modernisation processes as well as the disintegration and exclusion experiences owing to the deterioration of life circumstances, which questions educational justice and social participation, and thus can also constitute a risk for violent crime in childhood and adolescence.

2.

It then also touches on the discussion that **education is more than going to school**, to wit a continuous process in the course of life, and that, consequently, the educational formation processes of children and adolescents transpire at numerous locations in the course of growing up: at places of learning and living, the (educational) performances of which can evidently be taken for granted less and less for all adolescents, which is why these children also cannot draw on the relevant educational resources needed to ensure academic success.

These places of education, upbringing, supervision and care can also be **places of violence and prevention of violence** in the course of childhood and adolescence – and the strategies aimed at avoiding or reducing violence can also be defined from an educational angle. On the one hand, all forms of prevention focussed the individual place demands on education and are targeted at the development of the personality, the formation of identity and the acquisition of the ability to act. On the other hand, the predominant part of the strategies developed in recent years can be described as pedagogical strategies, which also consider violence in the course of childhood and adolescence as opportunities for learning and, as the case may be, also as an opportunity for providing pedagogical support.

3.

Thereafter, seen from the angle of "Places of education and prevention of violence" the **four places of education education** that are relevant for the upbringing of virtually all children – namely family, child day-care facilities, school, and offers and educational establishments of child and adolescent welfare – are analyzed with regard to their performance, opportunities and risks as well as with regard to their importance concerning the presence of **violence** and their strategies for the **prevention or reduction of violent crime**. These places are of equal importance and complement one another in their effects, which is also the reason why they are related to one another and should cooperate with one another.

3.1

Without a doubt, the **family** represents the primary lifeworld of children and adolescents. Although virtually all children do grow up in families, precarious developments are also to be found, as well as a great number of new challenges for fathers, mothers and children. These challenges also include the tasks of the family in the **educational process** of children. Never before has the central role of families been as evident as now. Not only was this clearly displayed by the PISA studies, but also the extent to which this success is dependent on their social situation and living conditions. Especially children from lower social classes and with a migrational background are underprivileged. Here the influence of the family is so great that it is extremely difficult to subsequently equalise inequalities by means of supportive systems and educational institutions. This gives rise to questions of whether and how the public responsibility can be strengthened with regard to the education of children, with the objective of supporting parental, relationship and educational competences – without intervening in the educational right of parents to raise their children.

Family upbringing and education does not always run smoothly and without any deficits – also at the risk of children becoming victims and perpetrators of **violent crime** or victims of violence within the family, owing to neglect, mental, physical and/or sexual abuse ("endangerment of welfare of children").

This violence toward children can give rise to significant subsequent problems which sustainably impact children's development. Thus, especially within the context of the family, programmes and measures aimed at **early prevention** are of considerable importance: statutory regulations such as the "condemnation of violence law", family planning offers and early assistance. However, also of importance is the fundamental

fostering of parental competences and behaviour by means of supportive and intervening measures, as well as the standard programmes for child and youth welfare.

3.2

The **child day-care facilities**, growing up in public responsibility, is one way of equalizing disadvantages by providing early access to publicly organized and operated places of education and education facilitating lifeworlds outside of the family. In recent years a fundamental change with regard to the assessment of the significance of **early childhood education and care** outside of the family has been noted. In the meantime, the child day-care facilities represent a lifeworld, which virtually all children in Germany experience – eventhough this might vary greatly with regard to the scope and quality.

One also cannot fail to note that, in the meantime, extremely high expectations are placed on child day-care facilities, which the facilities and the teachers working therein are presently unable to do justice to, when considering the currently applicable framework conditions. What definitely is true is that significant efforts will be required should one wish to attain child day-care facilities that are even remotely able to live up to the requirements and expectations placed in them. Apart from this, parents have to become increasingly and systematically more involved in the educational and upbringing processes of the child day-care facilities, for instance by means of the additional expansion of the number of child day-care facilities towards integrated and low-threshold accessible service and support systems ("Family Centres", "Early Excellence Centres").

As the first publicly organised and operated authority outside of the family, the child day-care facilities also represent a venue for the **prevention of violence.** This is particularly because they foster and support children and families in a very early stage as well as providing help. Additionally, they are in a position of providing protection against (potential) violence. For it is not violence among children or toward the caregivers that is the reason for measures of prevention of violence: in fact, there shouldn't be any "violence problem" present in child day-care facilities – not to mention the fact that even the use of the term "violence" for describing child behaviour is problematic and inappropriate.

Regarding (violence) prevention in child day-care facilities, the primary objective is to promote social competences; prevent or remove disadvantages and to support the integration and social participation of children. Apart from this, the target of the skilled personnel is to take over preventative tasks within the context of social early warning systems that have the purpose of recognising potentially problematic constellations with regard to the care and upbringing of a child as early on as possible.

3.3

Even though education is more than school, and successful life choices such as social integration build on the upbringing processes in families, child and youth welfare establishments as well as vocational education, there can be no doubt that **school** is the **central public place of learning** for children and adolescents in the process of growing up. The education gained in the course of school age plays a key role for the individual development; for participation in society and for imparting competences.

Not least because of this significance, school at the same time is also a strongly criticised place of education: the German school system does not appear to be providing the educational performance it should and which is expected of it. Neither is the entitlement to equal opportunities realized, nor that of a comprehensive general scholastic education.

Children and adolescents from socially weak classes are disadvantaged – and in recent years these "risk" classes have increased. A migrational background is a risk class that leads to disadvantages in all classes of the school system. The gender-specific discrimination against girls has in the meantime been abrogated; however, now there are new problem classes for boys. On the whole, the German school system is producing too many **educational losers**. Regardless of the aforementioned, all problems cannot be blamed on school, but also the upstream or complementing places of education such as the family, child day-care facilities and offers provided by child and youth welfare establishments. School, as the formal place of education can only function if the (non-formal) places of education function upstream and alongside it.

An answer to the undeniable problems of school education, which is the central educational political hope per se, is seen in the creation and expansion of **all-day schools throughout Germany**, not only in extending the number of hours in which the conventional schools are open, but also to complement these with other curricula and forms of learning. To which extent, however, the chance can be utilized of combining the strengths of the school with the strengths of other educational players, in particular with those of the **Child and Youth Welfare** is still largely unresolved. Just as unclear as the duration (and extent) of the conversion of the school system to all-day schools and the implementation of the "vision" of developing local alliances for education or communal educational landscapes

One of the demands placed on school as a public place of education is that it should do something about **violence and** the propensity of children and adolescents to violence. While school is seldom the "crime-scene" for juvenile violence, and there has been no general increase in physical violence and/or an increased level of brutality at school, it still is the place where children and adolescents dependably spend plenty of time and thus also, in principle, can also be reached by preventive measures and programmes.

Thus, on the one hand, strategies aimed at the **prevention of violence** at school have the objective of preventing violence or of reducing the violence which might flare up between school pupils. On the other hand they aim at having a positive influence on violence (or readiness to make use of it) among children and adolescents as a whole. Prevention of violence and the promotion of social competences are ongoing elements of school education and upbringing and are closely linked to **scholastic development**.

Here, in particular, it must be said that there is both a research gap and a need for research: to date, in the empirical studies concerning "violence at school", virtually without exception, research has only been done on violence of school pupils, and prevention programmes were only developed and deployed that were related hereto. Only rarely, if at all, has **violence of teachers** toward school pupils and the prevention hereof, been an issue.

3.4

Offers by the **Child and Youth Welfare** represent significant involvement in the educational trajectories of children and adolescents in the course of school-going age. This is in line with the mandate of Child and Youth Welfare for the fostering of personality development as well as contributing toward preventing or decreasing disadvantages and initiating and promoting educational processes.

Within the Child and Youth Welfare, it is especially the offers of the **Child and Youth work** that play a central role in the everyday life of children and adolescents, as extracurricular, predominantly non-formal learning locations. These enable educational processes based on active involvement and participation. Voluntariness and participation are firmly anchored fundamental principles of Child and Youth Welfare and can definitely impede cooperation with other partners, for instance with the school.

Within the context of youth work, the educational effects of **voluntary commitment,** by means of active cooperation in clubs, associations and initiatives are of importance. However, class-related differences can also be noted when use is made of these extracurricular learning locations. Indeed, the probability that adolescents will use these voluntary opportunities through active participation increases with their formal education.

Prevention is one of the structural principles of Child and Youth Welfare: Youth Welfare does not wait for impairments and injuries before it acts, but attempts to avert endangerment and dangers early on. **Prevention of violence** is just one of its tasks alongside others.

Here too the specific approach of Child and Youth Welfare is to be found in the principles of voluntariness and participation. Apart from this, it can also be seen in tying into the **resources and** not the deficits of young persons. Furthermore, it does not only focus on violent behaviour, but also looks at young people as a whole, who are accepted as persons. This does not, however, imply that their violent behaviour is also accepted. It is not unusual for Youth Welfare to come into a conflict between the different interests of adolescents and adults. One of their core tasks is to support adolescents in the event of such conflicts and to deescalate them, in particular with the purpose of viewing the adolescents' behaviour as appropriate for the age group and not to label it as "violence" too hastily. Also in the case of adolescents, who have already drawn attention to themselves with violent behaviour or have become delinquent, Youth Welfare does assume that educational approaches can contribute toward preventing violent behaviour.

Preliminary remark

"Education and qualification are the prerequisites for individual opportunities in life and participation in society ... for this reason, in a democratic state, educational justice must be given ... in Germany, however, this educational justice is not present: here educational success is highly dependent on one's social class and background."

The statement in the expert report pertaining to the main topic of the 14ᵗʰ German Congress on Crime Prevention 2009 "Live Solidarity - Secure Diversity" is based on findings of the social reporting at federal level, and here it particularly relies on the reports on education.[1] The problem of inequality owing to different backgrounds that was ascertained in these reports and in other empirical studies, and the associated discussion regarding equal opportunities and educational justice in Germany, was the occasion for making "Education – Prevention – Future" the main topic of the 15ᵗʰ German Congress on Crime Prevention in 2010, inasmuch as providing equal opportunities regarding access to education promotes integration and participation and thus also contributes toward the prevention of violence and criminality.

1
Life circumstances and opportunities in life in Germany

Today, as a result of societal modernisation processes, children and adolescents in Germany are growing up in a society which, owing to increasing disintegrational phenomena, is characterised not only by pluralization of lifestyles and attitudes toward values and objectives, but also by a growing socio-economic division, as well as an increasing scope of diversity with regard to social and ethnic-cultural aspects.

All reports and analyses, for instance on the risk of poverty because of the educational situation and the integration of migrants and their children, clearly show that the life circumstances have deteriorated significantly in recent years and decades for large parts of the population in Germany. More and more, society is drifting apart and the social disparities are becoming larger. Furthermore, problems with integration are increasing, and the social participation of entire parts of the populations is questioned.[2]

---

[1]   BBE 2006 and BBE 2008

[2]   Comprehensive details concerning the expert report on the main topic of the 14ᵗʰ German Congress on

1.1
Growing up in late modernism

The modernization of our society, characterised by

- functional differentiation
- individualisation and
- social disintegration

has brought chances as well as risks not only to society as a whole, but also to individuals. An individual's life and his or her private, professional and other opportunities are much less pre-determined at birth than used to be the case in the centuries before. In the **functionally differenciated** society there are no longer such clear roadmaps by which life courses are determined.

This **individualisation** provides individuals **chances** for personal independence and autonomy and offers the opportunity to actively shape their own lives. It does however also involve **risks**: breaking out from traditional ties can also result in uprooting, isolation and disorientation as well as increasing distances in social relationships – and it definitely does entail increasing **pressures to make choices and decisions**. Not only can individuals, to a great extent, determine their lives by themselves, they also have to – but not everyone is able and in a position to do this.

This is especially true if the individual's actual living circumstances (drastically) limit his or her respective **life circumstances**, social participation, integration into society – or, to be more precise: integration in the various societal functional areas and consequently also limit the chances that individualisation fundamentally brings.[3]

Children and adolescents are thus growing up "in a society which is characterised by the pluralization of lifestyles, attitudes toward values and goals and in which the social-structurally given objective opportunities in life present themselves in extremely different ways ... the associated requirements for successful life skills, as well as the learning and educational expectations placed on the subjects, pose new challenges for all children and adolescents as well as their families and pedagogical environ-

---

Crime Prevention 2009 "Live Solidarity - Secure Diversity" (Steffen 2009c) and, in the following, the "Hanoverian Declaration" of the 14th German Congress on Crime Prevention.

[3]   **Disintegration phenomena** are also highly visible at the social level. With growing commitment the question is being discussed as to how a society, which increasingly orients itself toward values such as self-realization and emancipation of individuals, can still be able to realise cohesion as a community of solidarity. In particular, there has been a rediscovery of **social inequality** and the associated destabilisation of life circumstances (Steffen 2009c). Against the background of the results of his current study on "German conditions", *Heitmeyer* expressly points out that numerous people fear that society will break apart and that social division as well as political resignation will increase. In particular, he sees opportunities to shape policy and to change these conditions in the municipalities in which these problems become visible (www.swp.de/hechingen/nachrichten/politik/art4306, 421629 ? of 27 March 2010).

ments. However, one must say that a great number of children and adolescents are capable of coping with the challenges without any major irregularities." But there is also a "… number of children and adolescents who cannot utilize the chances, who fail because of the risks and who are overtaxed" (Federal Ministry for Family, Seniors, Women and Youth (BMFSFJ)2009a, 45).[4]

1.2
Opportunities in life in precarious life circumstances

Although Germany continues to be one of the most prosperous countries in Europe, here too life circumstances are deteriorating; not only is income but also education and health increasingly unevenly distributed, disintegration experiences are also increasing, while the chances for social participation and integration are decreasing.

So, according to the third **Poverty and Wealth Report** the chasm between rich and poor has deepened; the uneven distribution of income has increased – and, particularly for children, also the risk of growing up in relative poverty. One quarter (26%) of the German population was affected by the risk of **income poverty** in 2005; social and family political transfer payments decreased this risk to 13%.[5]

The highest risk groups with regard to poverty are the unemployed, persons without completed vocational training, single parents and persons with migrational background – in each case this includes their children. Income and wealth do however have a decisive influence on the individual's options for action in society.

This is confirmed both by the **educational report** as well as the **health report**[6]: educational success, health prospects and the risk of children and adolescents contracting diseases still significantly depend on the social class and background. Especially adolescents of lower social groups and those with a migrational background are disadvantaged.[7]

---

[4]   *Keupp* (2009, 215) notes that "80 percent of adolescents integrate themselves well into life", asks "why actually?" and mentions "seven opportunities that children require": the sense of basic trust that is needed for living; dialectic of relatedness and autonomy; development of life coherency; creation of social resources by means of network formation; material capital as a prerequisite for relationship capital; democratic everyday culture by participation; self-efficacy experiences by means of commitment.

[5]   On the basis of his evaluations, the British social researcher Richard Wilkinson came to the conclusion that inequality is the cause of virtually all social problems in wealthy industrial countries and the greater the differences between rich and poor, the greater the social problems as well. Growing inequality divides society and wears it out – and politics contributes decisively to this development ((www.zeit.de/2010/13/Wohlstand-Interview-Richard-Wilkinson, of the 26th of March 2010.
In this regard, please also see the analyses and demands of the 8th Austrian Poverty Conference, which was held on the topic of "Social Investments Pay Off, for Everyone!" and took place in Salzburg on the 23rd/24th of February 2010 (www.ots.at/presseaussendung/OTS_0145/ergebnisse, dated the 25th of February 2010)

[6]   Especially in terms of the aspect of equal chances, the "Health of Children and Adolescents in Germany" has most recently applied itself to the 13th Children and Youth Report (Federal Ministry for Family, Seniors, Women and Youth (BMFSFJ)2009a).

[7]   In Germany, almost one fifth of the entire population has a migrational background, which need not be their migrational experience: Germany is the European nation with the most immigrants. Characteristic is the large degree of heterogeneity among the approximately 15 million people with a **migrational**

As it is, this **deterioration of life circumstances** exerts its **negative impact primarily on children and adolescents**. Income, education and integrational poverty lead to developmental disorders. Social class and background determine educational success and consequently integration and social participation. Disintegration and

Exclusion experiences can however facilitate violent crime. Or, in the accusatory words of Worten *Meyer-Timpes* (2008): "Poor children are highly endangered on their future way: poverty makes people sick; poverty keeps people stupid; poverty can turn a person into a criminal."[8]

Despite the aforementioned, one has to agree with *Keupp* (2009, 214), when he warns against scaremongering with regard to the adolescent generations and points out that the living conditions of families today, when compared to those of twenty or fifty years ago, have improved enormously. However: one group is hardly able to profit from the progress made in education and health and the improvements regarding safety and the opportunities in life. This is the group of children at the lower range of society; the families in which poverty, unemployment and neglect loom. And, this risk group includes one quarter to one fifth of all children.

Accordingly, the *13th Children and Youth Report* (Federal Ministry for Family, Seniors, Women and Youth (BMFSFJ)2009a, 45) stated the following: "Within the current societal changes one can see looming contradictory tendencies and this results in a situation in which "growing up today" becomes a constellation of "risky chances" … this is because the prerequisites for self-determined utilization of these chances … presupposes resources that are unattainable for numerous adolescents. Currently, the institutional resources from the educational system, the Child and Youth Welfare as well as the health system are only insufficiently able to compensate the person and

---

background, regardless of whether they are Germans or foreigners. Their life circumstances, possible integrational deficits and thus resulting integration needs differ significantly. If **successful integration** is understood to be the convergence of the living conditions of persons with migrational background to those of the native Germans in the sense of equal chances and equal participation, and if the persons with migrational background are classified by place of origin then these groups have clearly different levels of success. However, nowhere in Germany could one say that migrants are truly satisfactorily integrated (detailed, with further references, Steffen 2009c, Chapter 1.2.4).

[8]   At the **15th German Congress on Crime Prevention Ulrike Meyer-Timpe** will report on the topic of "What does Poverty mean within the Context of Educational Opportunities. The Consequences of Child Poverty burden Germany's Future – Perspectives and Concrete Proposals for Action."
A study of the OECD on the quality of children's lives draws the conclusion that, despite high government spending, child poverty in Germany is still very high in international comparison; here, every sixth child lives in relative poverty; in the OECD average it is only every eighth child (report in the Süddeutsche newspaper of 02.09.2009).
However, according to the Bundesjugendkuratorium (Federal Youth Board), in its statement on child poverty in Germany, child poverty does not inevitably have to lead to impediments. Numerous parents are successful at creating good prerequisites for their children's development, even though they might have a trying financial situation, and in virtually all such families the parents then cut down on their own spending to benefit their children (BJK 2009, 10ff.; also see FN 10).

milieu-related inequalities and to facilitate resources in such a manner that one would be in a position to speak about resource justness. Thus these resources also unintentionally contribute to increases in risk."

With the objective of creating such resources, on the 16th of February 2005, the federal cabinet adopted the **National Plan of Action** "For a Child-Friendly Germany 2005 – 2010" (NAP) and in spring 2008 launched the initiative "For a Child-Friendly Germany" in order to increase the political and public attention for child justice. Among other things the federal government sees a need for action in six areas of activity, including "Opportunity Justice by Education" and "Development of an Appropriate Living Standard for all Children."

In the 2008 interim report on the NAP, it was noted that the Federal Ministry for Family, Senior Citizens, Women and Youth had already been able to attain "decisive success on the road toward a child-oriented Germany".[9] *The Bundesjugendkuratorium (Federal Youth Board)*,[10] however, has a different view on this (2009, 4 and 16ff)[11]: despite political memoranda of understanding, a range of measures and political initiatives, until now, by no means could child poverty be sustainably reduced. The following measures for reducing child poverty are suggested[12]: the integration of mothers and fathers in the employment market, social transfers that move in the direction of ensuring basic security of children, the re-assessment of the Hartz-IV-standard rates[13], sustainable facilitation of disadvantaged children and families by means of infrastructure services and furthering of education, linkage of the great number of different local and regional providers of social services and educational measures for preventative networks.[14]

---

[9]   www.bmfsfj.de/BMFSFJ/kinder-und-ugend,did=31372,render=renderPrint.html of 11.05.2009 (query output: 28th of March 2010).

[10]   The Bundesjugendkuratorium (Federal Youth Board)(BJK) a committee of experts that has been deployed by the Federal Government to advise it in fundamental questions pertaining to Child and Youth Welfare and in cross-cutting issues of children and adolescent politics.

[11]   *Cathrin Kahlweit* is also critical: it is very difficult to reconcile the so-called "successes" with reality. "If the family minister were honest, she would admit that the National Plan for Action was already doomed to fail on the very day of its proclamation ... Can it be that when the National Plan of Action was drafted, child welfare was not the central concern? Many things that, theoretically at least, should be child-oriented are actually predominantly work-oriented ... everything purely economical considerations, which only marginally have anything to do with child welfare." (SZ Magazine No. 12 of the 26th of March 2010).

[12]   Similar suggestions have been made by the "Alliance for Fighting Child Poverty" (NRW state associations 2010).

[13]   In the meantime – with its ruling of the 9th of February 2010 – the Federal Constitutional Court decided that the regulations of the Social Security Code SGB II ("Hartz-IV-Law"), which determine the standard benefits of adults and children, do not comply with the constitutional right to provision of a humane existential minimum (press release No. 5/2010 on the 9th of February 2010).

[14]   An example for such a "chain of prevention" is the project "Mo.Ki – Monheim for Children"; in this regard see Hübenthal 2009.

1.3
Education, integration, participation: what about justness?[15]

Several years ago, the *Bundesjugendkuratorium* (Federal Youth Board) challenged educational policy to prepare itself for the (aforementioned) societal changes and their social impacts. They said that the education of the following generations is a key task for the future and that comprehensive education increasingly determines the degree of participation in society (BJK 2004b, 10). The *Federal Ministry for Education and Research agreed to this by introducing the* qualification initiative of the Federal Government's "Advancement through Education" (of January 2008) with the following words: "Education and qualification are the prerequisites for individual opportunities in life and participation in society" (BMBF 2009a)[16]. And in the *coalition agreement* between the CDU, CSU and FDP, dated 26 October 2009, the following was stated in chapter II. Education Republic of Germany: "Education is the prerequisite for comprehensive participation of the individual in the modern information society. Therefore, education is a civil right for us. For this reason we declare war on educational poverty." (2009, 59).

In the 21st century, education has become the most important key for social advancement and as such for the participation in social prosperity – in the meantime there is political consensus on this.[17] For this reason, in a democratic state such as Germany "educational justice" must be present: all members of our society must have the same opportunities regarding access to education in accordance with their abilities, regardless of their affiliation to certain groups. This educational justice is, however, not present in Germany: here the educational success is highly dependent on the social class and background - and this has a tradition.[18]

---

[15]   Thus the headline of the DJI Bulletin 81 PLUS (DJI 2008)

[16]   With regard to this "qualification initiative" two "educational summits" have already taken place between the Federation and the federal states: on the 22nd of October 2008 in Dresden and on the 16th of December 2009 in Berlin. The results were commented by Professor Wassilios Fthenakis, who is president of the Didacta association of education sector association as follows: "The educational republic of Germany is a poor country – poor regarding its political will to pay for the measures that are urgently required so as to secure the future of our children and to adapt the German educational system to international standards." (http://educationsklick.de/pm/71450/armes-reiches-land/ print version; query date: 29th of January 2010)

[17]   Education does not however only determine the development and prospects for action of every individual at work, in private life and as citizens, but also the sustainability of our society (BBE 2008, 6). According to a prognosis of the *CEPS* (Centre for European Policy Studies) in Brussels, when looked at from an economic viewpoint, Germany will fall behind significantly in international comparison. Shying away from reform and investments in education endangers prosperity: too many adolescents, especially migrant, leave school without having obtained their graduation certificate; today every fifth 15-year old German no longer goes beyond primary school niveau; this will not turn Germany into a high-tech state, but rather to a country of unskilled workers – Germany needs an expeditious education initiative (taken from an interview of the Süddeutsche Newspaper of 16 March 2010 with Daniel Gros, CEPS-head and co-author of the book "Nachkrisenzeit" ("Post Crisis Era")).

[18]   Educational justice is the antonym of educational discrimination. It's about equal educational opportunities, equal access to education, not about equal education. In this regard, please see "The DJI Bulletin 81" (Book 1/2008), which focuses on the topic of the 13th German Children and Youth Welfare Day

It is not just since PISA, IGLU and TIMMS[19] that the correlation between social origin and status in the educational system – or rather, the dependency of scholastic success on social class has been heatedly discussed in Germany: even though there can be no doubt that the expansion of education since the 1960s[20] has led to a rise in niveau in educational participation of the population, the "problem of inequality owing to origin and the thus ensuing discussion regarding equal opportunities and educational justice in Germany is a central theme in the education-sociological and educational-scientific discourse. On the basis of empirical studies, one can regulary prove significant differences in educational participation and scholastic success of children and adolescents, depending on gender, social origin, region and nationality, or migrational background" (Bos/Wendt 2008, 47).

But first and foremost, owing to the international educational-comparative studies (the so-called "PISA-Schock"), this topic has once again gained significance in the public discussion: although it is true that no participating country succeeded in de-coupling school pupils' performance from their social origin, nevertheless, in none of the participating countries was the correlation between social origin and, for example, reading competence as large as in Germany. This is particularly the case for children of migrants, who are identified as a special "risk group" by all these investigations time and again.[21] pronounced in Germany, in comparison to other societies. Then there are the difficulties of bi-cultural migrational situation, growing up and life in "another", "strange" cultural and social environment."

(18th – 20th of June 2008 in Essen) "Enable justness in Growing Up" and presents empirical results on the areas of "Education – Integration – Participation".

The view of Kraus (2008, 9f.) is similar: "At the start of their educational career everyone should – apart from their genes – have the same chances, but the same goal chances cannot exist ... anyhow, in education it is not about distributional justice in the sense of chances distribution, but rather about utilizing chances." In this regard, also see the annual expert report 2007 "Educational Justice" of the Action Council for Education, in which is stated: "educational justice is understood ... as the objective of organising the participation of society's members, regardless of disparities. Educational justice should not be confused with social justice ... educational policy must oppose the impression that educational justice leads to social justice." (2007, 135, 145).

[19] PISA: Programmes for International Student Assessment (www.mpib.berlin.mpg.de/pisa/); IGLU: Internationale Grundschul-Lese-Untersuchung (International Primary School Reading Study) (www.iglu. ifs-dortmund.de);); TIMMS: Trends in International Mathematics and Science Study (www.timms.mpg.de).

[20] The protagonists of the debate on opportunity inequality and educational justice included Georg Picht and his work published in 1964 – or rather: pamphlet – "The German Education Catastrophe", Ralf Dahrendorf and his plea "Education is a civil right" (1965) or also Hansgert Peisert and his analysis "Social Class and Educational Opportunities in Germany" (1967).

[21] Geißler and Weber-Menges (2008, 22) have come to the following conclusion in their analysis of the available data: "The children of migrants have a particularly difficult time in the German educational system: they are doubly disadvantaged. Owing to the strong tendency of segmentation of German society by migrants, many of them encounter the same problems with which native German children from socially weak families have to contend and which are especially strongly pronounced in Germany, in comparison to other societies. Then there are the difficulties of bi-cultural migrational situation, growing up and life in "another", "strange" cultural and social environment."

The findings of the *1st World Vision Children Study*[22] likewise document the increasing "culturalisation" and "inheritance" of inequality: "The weaker start chances of children from the lower social classes runs through all areas of life and is like a vicious circle. The risks of poverty and lacking resources are experienced as a burden and limit the possibilities of participation: in the family, which frequently is overtaxed by material pressure and existential concerns; at school, where the time and possibility for individual facilitation and promotion as an equalisation of disadvantages is generally lacking, as well as in the living environment or during leisure activities." For the *Bundesjugendkuratorium* (Federal Youth Board), the development of the educational system with regard to strengthening the principle of individual facilitation and support; the increase of the number of all-day school offerings and the link-up of forms of formal and informal education provide an "additional starting point for overcoming the inheritance of social inequalities" (2009, 30).[23]

2
Education is more than school
2.1
Education and places of education

If one follows the definition of the *12th Child and Youth Report*, education is "a comprehensive process of the development of a personality in the confrontation of oneself and one's environment. The subject is formed in an active co-construction or co-production process, adapts to the world and is dependent on educational opportunities, suggestions and encounters in order to develop and unfurl cultural, instrumental, social and personal competences" (Federal Ministry for Family, Seniors, Women and Youth (BMFSFJ) 2005a, 31).[24]

---

[22] The first World Vision-Children Study "Children in Germany 2007" is based on a representative random sample of 1,592 children ranging in age from 8 to 11 years. The children were personally interviewed and in addition there was a parents' questionnaire on the family background. The children's study complemented the Shell Youth Studies (www.shell.com/de-de/jugendstudie/), which are used at the age of 12 years and compiled by scientists of the University of Bielefeld and TNS Infratest Social Research in Munich. Conceptional foundation and contentual alignment of the study: Klaus Hurrelmann and Sabine Andresen. Commissioned by the world-wide operating children's aid associating World Vision Germany e. V. (http://www.worldvisionkinderstudie.de/die-studie-2007.html). In this regard also see Klaus Hurrelmann: socially weak children feel disadvantaged at an early age. Results of the 1st World Vision children's study (http://www.uni-bielefeld.de/gesundhw/ag4/projekte/worldvision.html)

[23] Against the background of his investigational results, *Heitmeyer* also demands equal opportunities in educational policy, which we are still a long way away from attaining. The worst is the finding that education in Germany is still inherited - and at the same time he warns against increasingly judging people according to their economic utility (www.swp.de/hechingen/ nachrichten/politik/art4306,421629? on 27 March 2010).

[24] Or, in the viewpoint of the coalition agreement between CDU, CSU and FDP (2009, 59): "Education is the prerequisite for internal and external freedom of mankind. It leads to intellectual independence, powers of judgement and awareness of values. Education is the prerequisite for comprehensive participation of each individual in today's modern knowledge society."

To form young persons in this manner was and is not the sole responsibility of school. Even though this institution does play a central role, education reaches far beyond school. The educational processes of children and adolescents take place at numerous **places of growing up**, both formal and non-formal[25]: Not only at school, but also in the family, at facilities and offers provided by the Child and Youth Welfare; in the group of persons of the same age; in the use of media, but also when visiting commercial recreational facilities; at tutoring services institutions; when travelling abroad or at a job (Federal Ministry for Family, Seniors, Women and Youth (BMFSFJ) 2005a, 32).

Education is thus (much) more than school; education is a continual process in the course of life.[26] Therefore the abilities a child brings along when it starts at school, are, among others the result of educational processes in the family and/or in establishments of child day-care facilities, which children can then draw on (DJI Bulletin 81 PLUS 2008, 1) – or, as the case may be, not.

For the forms of upstream education or non-formal or daily education that supplement school[27] are busy "becoming the actual key and future problem in the matter of education", given that their performance "can evidently be ensured less and less as a matter of course for all adolescents," (Rauschenbach 2009a, 87) – which is why these children then also cannot access the necessary education-relevant resources needed for success at school.

Successful all-day education (no longer) can be accepted as being self-evident. Formal education, school, can however only function if the education worlds upstream and alongside also function: "numerous things that are attributed to schools – both positive as well as negative, successes as well as failures – can in actual fact by no means exclusively or predominantly be attributed to it" ... "At any rate, one cannot simply deny that it is not formal education, but *everyday education, which to date has hardly been taken into account, which creates the chasm between privileged and the socially disadvantaged, between the educational beneficiaries and the educational losers*" (Rauschenbach 2009a, 86, 89).

In 2002 already, in its "Leipzig Theses" and also in 2004, in its position paper "New places of education for children and adolescents", the *Bundesjugendkuratorium (Federal Youth Board)* pleaded for a new understanding of education and pointed out

---

[25] Formal education is conducted in educational and schooling facilities and generally culminates in a recognised degree. Non-formal education takes place outside of the educational and schooling facilities for general and vocational education and does not lead to the acquisition of a recognised degree (BBE 2008, VIIf.).

[26] Thus, for example BJK 2002 and 2003; BBE 2008, 6; Rauschenbach 2009a, 25

[27] This is what Rauschenbach (2009a, 76, 83ff.) calls this important, but in its significance unrecognized, "other side of education." For him, **every-day education** is the part of the life-world bound educational event, in which it does not only refer to other educational venues, but also other learning modalities and educational contents.

the equal importance of the various kinds of places of education, both of the formal, non-formal and informal kind, as well as their complementary effects in the process of growing up – and raised the claim that every child should experience educational establishments such as child day-care facilities, school and offers of Youth Welfare organisations as spaces for learning and living, in which children's development – closely coordinated with the family – is promoted (BJK 2004b, 5, 13).[28]

For the *12th Child and Youth Report,* the findings that objectives, problem diagnoses as well as practise-oriented and political reform proposals for an improved exhaustion of societal education potentials no longer solely focus on the process of growing up *in*, but also *upstream and alongside school*, is the result of a cumulation of societal developments in the field of demography, economy and the employment market. Against the background that it is the duty of state and society, within the "public responsibility for growing up", to make it possible for adolescents to develop their lives themselves on the basis of their needs and to open up opportunities for acquiring competences, deliberations on converting and extending the system of education, care and upbringing have to link the requirements of society with subjective needs and abilities as well with the life circumstances of children and adolescents (Federal Ministry for Family, Seniors, Women and Youth (BMFSFJ) 2005a, 51f.).

2.2
Places of education as places of prevention of violence

Places of education, upbringing and care, and here in particular referring to family, child day-care facilities, school, Child and Youth Welfare offers and establishments are at the same time also venues where violence transpires and where violence can be prevented. As such they are strategic spheres for the prevention of violence[29] in childhood and adolescence.

Also understanding places of education as places of prevention applies without limitation to the three public sector instances, whilst the family as a private living space holds a special position. Given the development toward a (careful) strengthening of the public responsibility for the upbringing of children and the efforts undertaken in recent years for supporting familial education, also with the objective of condemning violence, the family as place of education is also analysed and discussed as a field of action for the prevention of violence.[30]

---

[28]   In this context, the *Bundesjugendkuratorium* (Federal Youth Board) points out in particular the necessity of cooperation between Youth Welfare and school, since such a comprehensive educational understanding can hardly be realised by the school in its classic form, as a teaching facility (more details on this in chapter 3.3).

[29]   Of course they also are fields of action for the prevention of crime in the course of childhood and adolescence in general. Owing to the considerable – also medial – significance given to "juvenile violence" and subsequent to the existing expert report for the German Congress on Crime Prevention, in particular with reference to the statement in the expert report for the 14th German Congress on Crime Prevention 2009 that violence is an indicator for social disintegration and lack of social participation, the focus will once again be on the prevention of violence.

[30]   So too the decision and explanation in the report of the Arbeitstelle (place of work) Child and Adolescent Crime Prevention of the German Youth Institute, which – as already in the preceding expert report – serves as

It might be surprising to describe strategies, programmes and measures for prevention of violence from the educational viewpoint. However, on the one hand, all forms of prevention focussed on the person **place demands on education** and are focussed on the development of the personality, the formation of identity or on acquiring the ability to perform. On the other hand, the greater part of the strategies developed in recent years can be characterised as being **pedagogical strategies**. This approach takes account of the fact that the prevention of violence in child and adolescent age has to do with people who are growing up, and who still have to develop their identity and moral awareness.

For that matter, for the most part, strategies are also then "pedagogical" and without a controlling or punishing focus when they bear on the behaviour of adults, for instance with regard to prevention of violence in the family.

The "pedagogic" view on violent actions also means understanding actual violence or the threat thereof, in the course of childhood and adolescence, as a **learning opportunity** and also, as the case may be, as an opportunity for pedagogical support. This does not, however, mean that this violence is to be accepted or that it should be downplayed. It does however mean that, in the first instance, prevention of violence is to be understood pedagogically and as a co-productive process: violence during childhood and adolescence primarily can and must be overcome by means of education, learning as well as acquisition of competency, and the sustainable prevention of violence can only be successful in cooperation with children and adolescents, with peers, parents, other responsible grownups or, as the case may be, the relevant social environment (Arbeitstelle (Place of Work) 2007, 281ff.).

Closely linked to this pedagogical viewpoint is the predominant position in specialist fields of practise to view acts of violence by children as only one and not the central aspect of their behaviour and rather to focus more closely on their competences, resources and the training of protective factors; in addition to take account of the respective social and cultural milieus, scenes and social areas (Arbeitstelle (Place of Work) 2007, 282).

However, this "pedagogical view" on violence and the prevention of violence harbours the danger of a "virtually inflationary extension of the understanding of crime and prevention of violence" per se, a dissolution of the boundary between the notions of violence and prevention, which among others could lead to general promotion programmes and measures of universal (also primary or social) prevention being re-labled to violence prevention programmes and measures. This "constriction" does not do justice to the significance of these programmes – and can have a discriminating impact on the target groups, which then again could compromise the use and effect of the programmes (Arbeitstelle (Place of Work) 2007, 16ff.).

---

an important foundation and reference (Arbeitsstelle Kinder- und Jugendkriminalitätsprävention 2007, 15).

Therefore, strategies, programmes, measures or projects are described as being **violence preventative** only if they directly or indirectly have the objective of preventing or reducing violence in the course of childhood and adolescence. Strategies for prevention of violence must justifiably and explicably have the primary purpose of preventing or reducing violence in childhood and adolescence – either on the foundation of convincing empirical evidence, experience or by means of plausible theoretical assumptions (Arbeitstelle (Place of Work) 2007, 17f.)

Thus strategies, programmes, measures and projects that are "violence preventative" can constitute **selective prevention** (also: situative or secondary) for special subgroups, individuals or even situations that are marked by relatively high risk factors, so that these persons stand under a heightened risk of becoming offenders or victims ("endangered persons as offenders and victims") or for situations where they are in danger owing to the fact that violent crimes might transpire ("opportunity for committing a crime").

Alternatively, they can have the purpose of **indexed prevention** (also: tertiary) and be aimed at those persons who have already become offenders and for whom, by means of the programmes and measures, an improvement of their future development is sought, or pertaining to situations in which criminal offences have already transpired more frequently ("criminal hot spots").[31]

3
Places of education and prevention of violence

If equal opportunities in education – educational justice – are viewed as one instrument for the **prevention of violence** and criminality among children and adolescents[32] then this would mean that, firstly, one would have to analyse the **learning and living spaces of children and adolescents** as places of education with regard to their performance, chances and risks, and that this is to be done in particular in terms of the aspect of successful/unsuccessful education. Secondly, this would mean demonstrating their relevance for the occurrence of violence, as well as their function as **fields of activity for** the prevention or decrease of violent crime during childhood and adolescence.

However, in doing so, one cannot go into detail with regard to all the abovementioned formal, non-formal and informal places of education – as that would go far beyond the scope of this expert report. Thus the four places of education have been selected that are relevant and of the same importance for the upbringing of virtually all children and which complement one another regarding their impact[33], which is also the reason

---

[31] For a more detailed report, see Steffen (2009c). This definition is also in accordance with the conviction that violence prevention strategies are only then justifiable if – at least when referring to public intervention – a threat or dangerous situations are at hand or substantiated, or that there is reason to fear that they might occur.

[32] So for instance in the programme "Innere Sicherheit, Fortschreibung 2008/2009" (Inner security, Update).

[33] Regarding the future perspectives for a publicly run, coordinated system of education, support and upbringing,

why they should bear upon one another and cooperate with each other: family, child day-care facilities, school and the offers and establishments of child and Youth Welfare organisations. [34]

3.1
Family as a place of education and prevention

The primary lifeworld of children and adolescents is the family. Regardless of the historical expansion of institutional and state-operated schooling and educational influences, the family is accorded a central role in the upbringing of children and adolescents ... Thus observation and analysis of the societal transformation of family structures and familial relationships is the central starting point for a future-oriented design of development and educational processes in the course of childhood and adolescence."
(Federal Ministry for Family, Seniors, Women and Youth (BMFSFJ) 2005a, 52).

3.1.1
Family as place of education

Virtually all children grow up in families. However, within society (not however in the official statistics) today the definition of "family" is much more encompassing than used to be the case still a few years ago: in comparison to survey results of the year 2000, in 2007 more people also consider unmarried parents and their children as well as single parent mothers or fathers as family (Federal Ministry for Family, Seniors, Women and Youth (BMFSFJ) 2009b, 32). According to *Peuckert,* the word "family" describes a life form that comprises at least one child and one parent and which displays a lasting relation, which is internally characterised by solidarity and personal closeness (2007, 36).[35]

In Germany, according to official statistics,[36] 13.8 million children live in 12.3 million families with children. More than half of the families (53%) have just one child, 11% have three and more children. Almost three quarters (74%) of the families living in Germany are married couples (with families with a migrational background, it is even 82%, with the families without migrational background, 71%). Of the families with

---

please see the remarks made in the 12ᵗʰ Child and Youth Report, in particular chapter 7 (Federal Ministry for Family, Seniors, Women and Youth (BMFSFJ)2005a) and here, in this expert report, chapter 3.3.1.

[34] There, for instance, the educational processes which result in the utilization and usage of **media** are not dealt with, even though the media have long already been a highly powerful (co)educator and, especially with regard to their impact on violence, have provoked heated discussion. However, firstly, media do not constitute a part of the aforementioned "aligned system of education, support and upbringing" and secondly, the "media topic" is so extensive that it alone could be the main topic of a future German Congress on Crime Prevention.

[35] Also for the *12ᵗʰ Child and Youth Report* these "close relationships", in which persons described as "family" live are a central criterion for constellations in which children grow up (Federal Ministry for Family, Seniors, Women and Youth (BMFSFJ)2005a, 113).

[36] Micro-census 2007 of the Federal Statistical Office, quoted in Federal Ministry for Family, Seniors, Women and Youth (BMFSFJ) 2009b, 32 ff.

more than one child, 85% of the parents are married, with the one-child families it is 66%. For approximately 100 years already, the share of the children growing up with both of their biological parents has remained constant at more than 80%.

Behind these findings one notices a change in the lifeworlds of childre and a variety of family forms that is not insignificant.[37]

While for the most part, children in Germany do grow up in familial situations that are in accordance with the traditional "normal concept"; increasingly however also in deviating family forms as well as in alternating familial constellations (Federal Ministry for Family, Seniors, Women and Youth (BMFSFJ) 2005a, 54; Bertram 2009).[38]

According to *Rauschenbach* (2009a 117f.), altogether, a rather **precarious development** is to be found in which the so popular picture of the happy and functional family is displaying first cracks: "the shrinking household sizes, the decreasing number of families, the decline in the number of children per family and the number of married couples with children; the undeniable instability of marital partnerships, the decreasing number of new marriages and birth figures, which has been a trend for many years already ... In the meantime, family as a life form has changed from a cultural matter of course to an individual choice."

The individualisation of lifestyles and the pluralization of lifeforms owing to the modernisation of society is "responsible" for this development.[39] Then there also are the "inner-family processes of change", primarily owing to the changing role of women, which is reflected in the increased share of female labour participation, especially in the share of labour participation of mothers.[40] In the meantime, the alleviation of the burden of combining family and job has become one of the family-political priorities of society (Federal Ministry for Family, Seniors, Women and Youth (BMFSFJ) 2009b).[41]

Hence, according to *Rauschenbach*, in the 21st century too, no alternative to the lifeform family is becoming apparent in contemporary society or has even established itself to a significant extent. Holding on to traditional images of families does however prevent finding the right answers to the new challenges of fathers, mothers and children (2009b, 3).

---

[37] This already makes clear the differences between East and West Germany (in this regard, see Federal Ministry for Family, Seniors, Women and Youth (BMFSFJ)2005a, 53).

[38] Thus, at the beginning of the 21st century for instance, the modern small family, as represented by the community of married parents with their biological children is only one of numerous family forms, even if it is the most important (Peuckert 2007, 36).

[39] See above chapter 1.1; and also Peuckert 2007, 36,48; Rauschenbach 2009a, 121 and 2009b; Schwind 2009.

[40] Data and figures regarding this can be found at Peuckert 2007, 48ff.

[41] In this regard also see the demands of the time researcher *Ulrich Mückenberger* for a "contemporary political change": mothers and fathers have to be granted the legal right to temporarily reduce their working time – without having to forego career opportunities (2009, 10).

Among these challenges are also the tasks of the family in the **educational process of children**. For: it is within the family where everything starts for children – also as regards education (Rauschenbach 2009a, 124). Within this context, the *12th Child and Youth Report* stated that family offers the decisive context for cognitive, emotional and lingual development of most children, for their social and personality development as well as for their physical and psychological health. Thus the family has a decisive influence on the course of development of the educational processes of children (Federal Ministry for Family, Seniors, Women and Youth (BMFSFJ) 2005a, 114).

However, parental relationships and educational competences, and their development and implementation in concrete daily educational measures cannot be detached from the conditions in which families do, want to or have to shape their lives: to be mentioned in this regard are their economical and time resources[42], the organisation of care-taking arrangements for children outside of the family or in cooperation with the school (Federal Ministry for Family, Seniors, Women and Youth (BMFSFJ) 2005b, 15).

Not only did the **PISA-studies**[43] make the central role of family on the success of the following generations' learning and educational processes clearer than ever before, but also the extent to which this success depends on their social class and living conditions. In Germany, more than in any other country that participated in the PISA studies, the pupils' success is dependent on their **social background**. And not only with regard to the thus involved economical and time resources, but also on the equally dependent familial bonding and educational processes of the family environment (socio-spatial), of the facilitation within and through the family.[44]

Especially disadvantaged are adolescents of lower social groups and those with a migrational background.[45] Children with at least one parent born abroad, and even if these families have the same socio-economical status, less frequently attend high school and are more frequently to be found in the lower-qualified kinds of schools than native

---

[42]   Regarding the impacts of invisible working relationships, competitive pressure or the fear of social decline on everyday family life, see Lange/Jurczyk 2009.

[43]   See above FN 19.

[44]   The *12th Child and Youth Report* stated as follows: "There are significant differences in the life circumstances of children, depending on their family background, level of education, socio-economic position, cultural and ethnic affiliation as well as the regionally given circumstances. A great many dimensions thus determine the life circumstances, in particular the education and training level, employment status, health, living situation and environment, the family situation and the social networks, as well as income and wealth." (Federal Ministry for Family, Seniors, Women and Youth (BMFSFJ) 2005a, 118).

[45]   In this regard, see above, Chapter 1 on the "influence of particular life circumstances" such as income poverty, migration and socio-spatial conditions, also see Federal Ministry for Family, Seniors, Women and Youth (BMFSFJ)2005b, 118ff. On the living conditions of adolescents with a migrational background, in particular regarding their everyday life, also see Uslucan 2009 and Thiessen 2009.
    Haci-Halil Uslucan will speak at the **15th German Congress on Crime Prevention** on the topic of "Unrecognised Potentials: Educational Participation and Facilitation of Education of Adolescents with a Migrational History."

German pupils (BBE 2008, 62 f).[46]

This disadvantage also becomes apparent with regard to the pupils' level of cognitive competences (in the areas of reading, mathematics and natural sciences).[47] While it appears that there has been some success in somewhat reducing the competence-level differences owing to the children's background, school children with a migrational background are still clearly lagging behind: "All in all, ultimately, the facilitation of children and adolescents with a migrational background remains insufficient." (BBE 2008, 85)[48]

The family is not only of central importance – both positively as well as negatively – with regard to the educational process of children, but, according to *Rauschenbach* (2009a, 123), this "course-setting influence of family" obviously has a much more significant impact on the life and educational opportunities of adolescents than can subsequently be evened out by supporting systems and educational institutions. Or, in the words of the *Scientific Advisory Board for Family Issues*: the family has to be recognised and strengthened as a place of education if subsequent measures of educational promotion and facilitation are not to be in vain (Federal Ministry for Family, Seniors, Women and Youth (BMFSFJ) 2005b. 5).

This intensity of the family as a place of education makes it difficult to subsequently even out inequalities – at least with the means offered by the current-day education and social policies – and this is especially owing to the fact that the family represents the primary relationship and educational context (BMFSFJ, 2005b, 9), the "first, longest-lasting and least thematically selective, whilst at the same time most time-intensive place of growing up", in which, additionally, the triad of *care-taking, upbringing and education* are anchored. Since, for children, family is the place where everything comes together, deficits and risks in the course of care-taking, upbringing and education can also have grave effects (Rauschenbach 2009a, 124ff.).

In view of the established deficits and disadvantages, *Rauschenbach* (2009a, 133f.) advocates carefully strengthening **public responsibility for** the upbringing of children, with the objective of "thus supporting families and integrating them into a learning, care-taking and education network so as to place them in a position of doing

---

[46] Such background-based differences can also be recognised with regard to the **utilization of learning locations outside school** – for instance with the offers provided by child and youth work and in particular with regard to the participation (voluntary commitment) in clubs, associations and initiatives (BBE 2008, 80). Thus the learning locations outside school do not fulfil the expectations placed in them pertaining to the equalisation of disparities with regard to equal access to learning opportunities in school settings. In this regard, also see Chapter 3.4.

[47] Since the mid 1990s there have been systematic investigations in Germany regarding which learning results are attained at the "central hinges" of the schooling system. Statements regarding this were already contained in the Education Report 2006, with a chapter on the "Significance of Migration on Education".

[48] How one can ensure equal opportunities for children with a migrational background, is illustrated by the education authority in Toronto / Canada (Article "World Champion of Integration" in DIE ZEIT (newspaper) No. 35 of 21 August 2008).

justice to their fundamental responsibility of bringing up their children, even under the significantly changed conditions of current societies, and that this can be done without them being burdened by the ever more unfulfillable expectation that they should and have to be able to take care of everything themselves ... therein lies the actual challenge of the state and society: not to relieve families from their responsibility, but to empower them ... The family should be recognised as a life form which one can best strengthen by firstly, pragmatically, taking note of its actual situation, yet at the same time, secondly, also realising that its stability, which has been regarded as eternal, has sufficiently often become fragile and, thirdly, in particular, that one can assist the family by creating and expanding family-friendly infrastructure services."[49]

The *Scientific Advisory Board for Family Issues* also advocates the strengthening of parental relationships and educational competences, does however expressly refer to the "natural" right of parents to bring up their children, which has constitutional status,[50] which is why the state also cannot impose a certain educational style on parents, but can only recommend and facilitate a certain educational behaviour. The advisory board sees it as promising to develop **educational offers** for parents and to make these easily accessible; what is however of importance for the advisory board is the principle of **voluntary** participation in these offers. The role of national institutions can only relate to the expansion of the offers and the guarantee of their diversity, not however to making their contents binding[51] Further, the advisory board also advocates the formation and care of **upbringing partnerships**, for the coordinated cooperation of all persons and institutions involved in upbringing, in particular of the educators at child day-care facilities and teachers at schools. For the advisory board, **participation** is of importance as well as the possibility for parents (and also for children) of being able to give their opinion in the respective establishments and to have a firm place in the processes involved in decision-making (Federal Ministry for Family, Seniors, Women and Youth (BMFSFJ) 2005b, 24ff.).

However, according to the Board, the **dilemma** is that the very parents who should most urgently take a self-critical look at their educational skills, normally have poor prerequisites for doing this – and that there are problematic situations in which experts should actually intervene, which then results in parents occasionally no longer being the key actors in the educational process of their children, be it for a limited or perhaps even indefinite period of time (Federal Ministry for Family, Seniors, Women

---

[49] In this regard, also see Bertram 2009 and Chapter 3.2.

[50] In Article 6, Paragraph 2 of the Constitutional Law of the Federal Republic of Germany the following is stated: "care and upbringing of children is the natural right of parents and the duty that first and foremost is incumbent upon them."

[51] "Parental testimonials, even such that are connected with sanctions in the event of "insufficient" performances (e.g. cuts in child allowances) are an unsuitable and also quite tenuous tool for improving parental competences and attaining more responsible parenting." (Federal Ministry for Family, Seniors, Women and Youth (BMFSFJ) 2005b, 26)

and Youth (BMFSFJ) 2005b, 29).

3.1.2
Family as place of prevention of violence

Hence, upbringing within the family is not always free of trouble and deficits. The *12ᵗʰ Child and Youth Report has* even come to the conclusion that, less and less, it can be assumed that the right and duty involved in the upbringing of children by their parents is implemented as ably as it is deemed to be self-evident (Federal Ministry for Family, Seniors, Women and Youth (BMFSFJ) 2005a, 49).

As shown, the developments within society have an impact on families and their care and support, upbringing and educational performance. In our society, which is highly differentiated socially, ethnically and culturally, deficits and problems can jeopardise the development of children as autonomous persons with the capacity of acting in a community – also with regard to the risk of them becoming victims or perpetrators of (violent) crime (Steffen 2009a).

In order to prevent or at least alleviate this risk, the support of public instances such as child day-care facilities, Youth Welfare, school, police and justice is needed. Clearly they are responsible for the prevention of violent crime in the course of childhood and adolescence, whilst the family, as a private sphere, plays a special role. However, within the context of the aforementioned demand for the careful strengthening of the role of public responsibility in the upbringing of children, apart from the private responsibility of the parents, more focus should be placed on increasingly viewing the **"public responsibility for the prevention of violence"** as a responsibility and challenge for the entire society. This too before the background that, in recent years, a multitude of endeavours have been undertaken to support upbringing within the family, also with the objective of "condemnation of violence" (Arbeitsstelle Kinder- und Jugendkriminalitätsprävention 2007, 15).

Deficits in respect to familial support, upbringing and education can not only contribute toward children and adolescents becoming victims and perpetrators of violent crime during the process of growing up. They can also have the effect of children and adolescents directly and proximately becoming victims of violence within the family by means of (parental) neglect or physical, psychological and/or sexual abuse ("endangerment of the child's well-being") and/ or indirect victims of the acts of violence between the parents or legal guardians ("endangerment of the children's well-being with cases of intimate partner violence").[52]

---

[52]   Regarding the definition, scope, impact and prevention of these forms of violence within the family see Galm and others 2007; Heynen 2007; Kindler 2007; Buskotte 2007. Also see "Facts and figures on child neglect and abuse", Nationales Zentrum Frühe Hilfen (www.fruehehilfen.de/3334.98.html) (National Centre for Early Help) and Wetzels 2009.

Investigation findings indicate that the majority of endangered children are not exposed to only one form of violence, and also that children who have already become victims of violence run a high risk of being victimised once again. Other significant risk factors are partner violence[53], affirmative support of harsh punishment and rejection of the child (Galm and others 2007, 35f.).

It goes without saying that violence against children is to be condemned as a matter or principle. This also holds true because violence can lead to considerable **follow-up problems**, which "can display a variety of different forms, depending on the type and severity of the endangerment of the children's well-being within the context of the child's further life reality." As has been demonstrated, among other things, there are adverse effects on the child's emotional and cognitive development and the development of its interests, and these in turn can induce conflicts in child day-care facilities and schools, as well as school achievement disorders. Especially with boys, experiencing violence can form the backdrop for a boy's own delinquency and propensity to use violence himself (Galm and others. 2007, 37f.; Heynen 2007, 62).

Neuro-biological research has drawn attention to the extent to which early childhood experiences, particularly severe psychological stress in early childhood can impact the subsequent physical and social-emotional development, right up to psychological illnesses or violent crime, and in some cases even irreversibly (Bundesarbeitsgemeinschaft 2009, 13; Lucas 2009; Roth 2008, 11). This research has also fundamentally substantiated that, independently of such stress experiences, it is especially the early years that are of decisive importance for the further development (Hüther and others 1999).

Hence, especially within the familial context, the **importance of early prevention** is obvious – in order to prevent a situation arising in which the children's well-being is at risk or at least to improve the protection of children and adolescents regarding risks for their welfare.[54] In this regard one should distinguish between universal prevention strategies that have their principal focus on all parents; selective strategies aimed at

---

[53]   For a long time, hardly any attention was paid to the situation of children and adolescents who have been affected by domestic violence (partner violence), be it directly or indirectly. In the meantime, however, domestic violence is seen as a serious criterion for threats to a child's well-being, and even the lawmakers have extended the possibilities for protection: the police laws of the Federal states regulate the powers of the police to remove violent persons or order them to leave, the law providing protection against violence enables, for example, the assignment of joint living quarters to one of the parents or guardians, and stalking legislation can also have a positive impact. One of the tasks of the Youth Welfare office is to investigate a possible threat to the child's well-being owing to having witnessed violence, to mediate further help and, as the case may be, also to initiate proceedings before a family court (Heynen 2007, 64ff.; Buskotte 2007).

[54]   Thus the amendment of § 8a of the Social Security Code VIII, which came into force on 01.10.2005, "Protection mandate regarding endangerment to children's well-being" dealt with the elaboration of the process for prevention of a directly threatening risk for children's well-being, for which "important indications" already exist and as such no longer refers to the early recognition of risk factors and threats (Galm and others 2007, 40)

parents with low relationship and upbringing competences as well as those that have already developed an inappropriate parental rearing practice and finally, indicated strategies are employed when disorders or deviations that are to be evaluated critically have already occurred within the child's upbringing and are related to problematic parental upbringing practice (Federal Ministry for Family, Seniors, Women and Youth (BMFSFJ) 2005b, 22f). However, these distinctions cannot always be drawn clearly: the boundaries between the prevention strategies are fluent in the same manner as are those between normality, stress and threats to a child's development. The parents' need for support can range from providing information, offering targeted support and guidance right up to the prevention of threats to the child's well-being, and the respective programmes and measures can indeed pursue different prevention strategies.

The **universal prevention strategies** include, for example, the "Law on Condemnation of Violence in Upbringing", which went into effect almost ten years ago, on 02.11.2000[55]. The thus amended §1631, Paragraph 2 of the German Civil Code clearly now reads: "Children have a right to non-violent upbringing. Physical punishment, mental abuse and other degrading measures are not permitted." The order commissioned by Federal Ministry for Family, Seniors, Women and Youth (BMFSFJ)and the Federal Ministry of Justice (BMJ) for *accompanying research* on the impacts of the this law on condemnation of violence, constitutes a positive change in the attitudes on non-violence which has to date, however, only established itself to a limited extent in everyday upbringing. In particular, in the families burdened by violence, the use of physical violence has not decreased and the number of these families has also hardly changed (Bussmann 2005).

This is in line with findings by the *KFN-surveys of school children (KFN: Criminological Research Institute of Lower Saxony),* according to which parental violence toward their children has not consistently decreased; especially the severe forms of violence were still just as prevalent in 2005 as in 1998 (Baier and others 2006, 43). However, the surveys conducted by KFN in 2007 and 2008 were able to establish that fewer adolescents had to endure parental violence and that, in particular in cities, the quota of children being brought up in an entirely non-violent manner had clearly increased (Baier and others 2009). For *Erthal/Bussmann,* the results of a European comparative study that was conducted by them in 2007/2008 suggest that "a law banning corporal punishment does have an influence in decreasing violence"; for Germany, since 1996 a continual decline in the legal approval of violence in the course of upbringing could be observed (Erthal/Bussmann 2009, 53).

---

[55] Again, ten years before that, in 1990, a corresponding regulation was already demanded by the "Violence Commission" of the Federal Government (Schwind/Baumann and others 1990). Internationally, the right to a non-violent upbringing was already codified in 1989 in Article 19 of the UN Convention on the Rights of Children. Already ten years prior to this, in 1979, Sweden was the first European state to anchor such a right in law (Erthal/Bussmann 2009, 37).

There is also a variety of offers with rather universal appeal for the **education of families**.[56] Thus, for example, **parent training programmes** have the purpose of facilitating parental rearing practise, are for the most part offered in group rounds and include a structured sequence of training sessions that frequently deal with exercises pertaining to positive educational practises, mediation of social rules and manners to deal with problematic children behaviour.[57] On average, the parent training programmes do display a high level of efficiency and in part also achieve better effects than the so-called social training programmes for children.

However, with regard to these programmes, the problem frequently occurs that it is very hard to win over parents from high-risk families and burdened contexts to participate in such programmes or that they frequently drop out of the courses (Beelmann 2009, 261f.).[58]

The *selective prevention strategies* – at least for the most part – include the so-called **"early help"[59] systems; which are** local and regional supporting systems with coordinated offers of assistance for parents and children, starting with pregnancy, and continuing into the early years. Here the special focus is on the age group of 0 to 3 year-olds. These strategies have the objective of sustainably improving the possibilities for the development of children and parents in family and society early on in life.

Apart from support in the field of everyday practical skills, early help particularly wants to contribute toward facilitating the relationship and rearing competence of (expectant) mothers and fathers. Thus it provides a significant contribution for the healthy rearing of children and secures their rights to protection, fostering and participation ... Fundamental are offers that are aimed at all (expectant) parents with their children, in the sense of health support. In addition to this, early help is particularly aimed at families in problematic situations (selective prevention). Of central significance for the practical implementation of early help is ... close networking and cooperation of institutes and offers in the fields of pregnancy counselling, the public health sector, the interdisciplinary early support programmes of the Child and Youth Welfare and additional social services ..." [60]

---

[56] Examples of this, with short descriptions, can also be found at Sann / Thrum 2008 and at Lösel 2006.

[57] Examples of this are the Triple-P-Programm (www.triplep.de) and the programme "EFFEKT – development facilitation within families: parents and children training", to-date the only combined development and prevention study in Germany (University of Erlangen-Nürnberg) Lösel and others (2008 and 2010).

[58] In this regard, also see the "Inventory and Evaluation of Offers in the Area of Parental Education", which *Lösel* conducted on behalf of the Federal Ministry for Family, Seniors, Women and Youth (BMFSFJ), (status November 2006); available via publikationen@bundesregierung.de

[59] Definition according to www.fruehehilfen.de/4010.0.html

[60] For a critical view of "early help as a perfected controlling system" see Keupp 2009. See also Sann/ Schaefer 2008.

Since March 2007, within the context of the Programme of Action of the Federal Ministry for Family, Seniors, Women and Youth (BMFSFJ), the Federal Centre for Health Education (BZgA) and the German Youth Institute (DJI) have been providing "early help for parents and children and social early warning systems" in joint sponsorship with the *National Centre for Prevention of Neglect and Maltreatment in Early Childhood (NZFH)*. [61]

The centre provides practical support in recognising familiar burdens earlier on and more effectively and by providing supporting offers in accordance with demand. The NZFH's higher ranking goal is to better protect children against danger earlier on by means of an effective networking of early help systems of the public health sector and the Child and Youth Welfare, whereby this goal is to be attained primarily by improving the accessibility of risk groups.[62].

The supported pilot projects have been evaluated; initial results are available. Owing to the short duration of the evaluation, a sustainable impact cannot however be proven yet. But it has become apparent that far fewer families can be reached by the pilot projects than was originally planned (DJI 2009d, 46).

Already prior to the establishment of the NZFH, both at *community* as well as at *state levels*, it was possible to recognize definite activities with the aim of increasingly focussing on providing early and preventative help; in the meantime these offers have been expanded even more.[63] Most of these approaches are selectively applied, thus are aimed at families with an increased risk of abuse and neglect. With these so-called (high) **risk families** the living conditions are already burdened by numerous negative conditions and risks, which evidently still mutually complement and reinforce one another. These risks include, for example, poverty, lacking social support in the family, biographical burden of the parents (for instance that the parents themselves had been abused or neglected in their childhood) psychological illnesses and alcohol and substance abuse (Bundesarbeitsgemeinschaft (Federal Work Group)/ 2009, 12).

---

[61]   www.fruehehilfen.de/3232.98.html; in this regard, also see a first rating of this centre by von der Leyen 2009.

[62]   In this regard, also see the expertise commissioned by the NZFH on the international status of research of impact (Lengning/Zimmermann 2009), the extremely informative statement of the German Youth Institute on the topic "New Concepts Early Help" (DJI 2009d), as well as the symposium "Interdisciplinary early support in the system of early help" from the 22nd to the 23rd of March 2010 in Kassel-Wilhelmshöhe.

[63]   In this regard, see Galm and others 2007; the magazine 1-2/2005 of the IKK-news "Violence against Children: Early Recognition – Early Help" (Information Centre Child Abuse / Child Neglegt of the German Youth Institute e.V.) as well as the National Action Plan "For Germany, Fit for Children 2005 – 2010", in which the topic of "Growing up without violence" is in focus. Already in the coalition agreement of November 2005, the coalition fractions of the CDU, CSU and SPD have already thematised the early support of children who are at risk. In the coalition agreement of the new Federal Government of 26 October 2009, in Chapter III "Social Progress" the issue of "children protection and early help" was mentioned and the intensification thereof is given as an objective.

Family-oriented **early prevention concepts** pursue the aim of recognising problematic careers as early on as possible and, in the tradition of the socio-pedagogical early support and compensatory pre-school upbringing, they consist of different offers of help and support for children up to the age of six, and their families. Pertaining to the effectivity of these programmes, there are evaluations, some of which are very comprehensive with long follow-up periods of time, where, among other things, the subsequent delinquency and criminality served as criteria for defining success (Beelmann 2009, 262). [64]

Apart from these strategies that are focussed on early recognition and support, there also are numerous **support and intervention measures** aimed at basic facilitation of parental competences and behaviour. These approaches, which are focussed on parents and families, try to reduce the risk of a dissocial development of children and adolescents, by means of systematic education, support and assistance for parents and families.

The *indicated prevention strategies* include, for example, the *standard offers of the child and Youth Welfare*: aids for upbringing that aim to guide and support parents in an appropriate manner, say in the context of educational and family counselling support or social-pedagogical family support.[65] Child-related support focuses on individual support and/or needs for treating children or adolescents and should even out negative impacts in the course of their development in addition to strengthening their psycho-social and cognitive competences. If parents are not willing or able to accept the support offered or to alter their style of upbringing, steps can be initiated to involve the Family Court (Galm and others 2007, 42). [66]

---

[64] One of the best known programmes of this kind is the **Perry Preschool Study**, for which "particularly disadvantaged" children in the age bracket of 4-5 years were selected in Ypsilanti, Michigan, USA in 1962. It was possible to establish that almost 35 years after going through this programme, the children who were a part of it displayed, among others, a significantly lower number of convictions and imprisonment for criminal offences (Beelmann 2009, 262). However, not only are these effects known, but also the cost-benefit-analysis to which the Perry Preschool Study was subjected: For each preschool child, there was a net profit of almost 250,000 dollars (in this regard also see the script of the broadcast "Research and Society" in Deutschlandradio Kultur of 26 February 2009; Sybille Salewski: learning pays off. The economist James Heckmann calculates the value of early childhood education). **Peter Lutz** will speak at the **15th German Congress on Crime Prevention** on the topic of "Preschool education pays off – the example of the Perry Preschool Project".**Meinrad Armbruster** will speak at the **15th German Congress on Crime Prevention** on the topic of "ELTERN-AG: a prevention programme of early parents' education for the socially disadvantaged".

[65] Criticism regarding the - insufficient – personnel situation in Child and Family Guidance Counselling Menne 2009

[66] Sanctions are also being considered by, for example, the *CDU Baden-Württemberg* at their party conference in November 2009, where they demanded that the state aid for parents who neglect their children be decreased. Hartz IV-recipients, who do not look after their children well enough, should be subjected to sanctions (Süddeutsche Zeitung of 23 November 2009). An opposing attitude is taken by the *Scientific Advisory Board for Family Policy Issues*, and does not deem "parent testimonials, even combined with sanctions" as the appropriate measure for increasing parental competences (Federal Ministry for Family, Seniors, Women and Youth (BMFSFJ) 2005b, 26; also FN 51

With regard to the **effectivity** of the programmes and measures of the **selective and indicated prevention strategies** *Beelmann* comes to the overall appraisal that: "with due caution, we can state that development-psychological and evidence-based programmes on the prevention of violence and criminality do exist such as, say, social training programmes for children, parent training programmes or early family-oriented measures for high-risk groups." (2009, 269). [67]

3.2
Child day-care facilities as place of education and prevention

"Elementary education is the task of the family, but not only a private matter ... elementary education is a task for society and thus also requires public accountability."
(BJK 2004a)

3.2.1
Growing up in public responsibility

If the development and educational chances of children are significantly determined by their family background, the facilitation of educational justice can also imply that the disadvantages are to be evened out by early access to publicly organised and operated places of education and education promoting lifeworlds outside of the family. Then, growing up in public responsibility means that all children are afforded access to optimal perspectives – regardless of how much they acquire at home. [68]

The first publicly organised and operated places of education outside of the family are the **child day-care facilities** [69]; these include the day-care facilities for children such as crèches, kindergartens and the like as well as child day-care. [70] Visiting these establishments for early childhood education should contribute to more justice *among*

---

[67]   However, it is especially the aids used by the Child and Youth Welfare in the event of suspected or actual intra-family violence against children **that have not been systematically evaluated** (Galm and others 2007, 43). Hence the statement to be found in the *coalition agreement* between the CDU, CSU and FDP of 26 October 2009 is to be welcomed (S. 71): "We shall review the Child and Youth Welfare system and its legal bases in the Social Security Code (SGB) VIII with regard to its accuracy and effectivity. We want early, speedy and unbureaucratic accesses to assistance by highly qualified service offerings and the elimination of interface problems between the Youth Welfare and other systems that provide assistance. This applies particularly to the early help systems and other help systems for young persons with disabilities. We shall evaluate the quality of the Child and Youth Welfare and, as the case may be, perfect and develop standards."

[68]   In this regard see DJI Bulletin 80, 2007, 33 and Bock-Famulla 2008, 6.

[69]   Child day-care belongs to Child and Youth Welfare and is a part of social legislation, as regulated in the Social Security Code (SGB) VIII, the Child and Youth Welfare Law. Child day-care falls within the jurisdiction of the municipalities through the local Youth Welfare offices; de facto, however, it is rendered with a share of way over 60% by non-governmental sponsors, the so-called "private sponsors", frequently denominational sponsors of the Roman Catholic and Evangelical churches in Germany (Sommerfeld 2007, 74f.; Rauschenbach 2009, 138f.).

[70]   Child day-care is a family-based, flexible type of care by day care attendants – for instance a child minder – especially for children under the age of three (DJI Thema 2009/02). Regarding status and challenges also see Jurczyk/Heitkoetter 2007.

children and by means of early facilitation it should also increase the future chances for *all* children (DJI Bulletin 81, 1/2008, 11).

Not only is this assessment of the significance of **early support of children** in line with the insights of neurobiology[71], but also with those of the economics of education.[72] Since the early access to education and education promoting lifeworlds can have a positive influence on the entire educational biography, it would definitely make more sense and be more efficient to invest early on, rather than paying for repairs and follow-up costs later on (Bock- Famulla 2008, 6).

The *12th Child and Youth Report also* focuses on the "obvious backlog demand" in Germany "with a view to its offer for public education, care and rearing": "for too long and too one-sidedly has the former Federal Republic virtually exclusively relied on family and school as the unquestionably given supporting pillars of childhood and adolescence. In doing so, the family in particular was responsible for the care and upbringing of the children and the school for the education" (Federal Ministry for Family, Seniors, Women and Youth (BMFSFJ) 2005a, 28 f).

In recent years, however, the publicly organised and operated place of education "child day-care facilities" has experienced so much transition that a **fundamental change in the understanding of the significance of early childhood education and care outside of the family** can be established: "For Germany the child day-care facilities have proven to be a child-political setting of course" (DJI Bulletin 80, 2007, 33).[73]

---

[71] In this regard see, e.g. the remarks by Bergmann/ Huether 2009 and Huether 2009 "Why does the brain become the way one uses it." Only in the last 10 years have brain researchers and development psychologists been successful in proving the extent in which the structuring of the brain depends on how and for what purpose a child uses its brain. At the time of birth the human brain is still highly unfinished. Virtually everything that impacts later life still has to be learnt and stored within the brain as a new experience (Bergmann/Huether 2009, 68f.). Our brain creates networks, thinks and works in the manner in which we use it and new connections are always then created very quickly and are extremely tightly linked together, when the things we intensively occupy ourselves with, are of particular significance for us (Huether 2009, 59)
Gerald Huether will speak at the opening plenary session of the **15th German Congress on Crime Prevention** on the topic of "What shapes us, knowledge or experience?"

[72] According to insights of the **economy of education, by trend,** the yields of investments in education tend to decrease with increasing age. Especially for children from socially disadvantaged classes the yields have a tendency of being higher in the early childhood (Wößmann 2008). In this regard also see the research results of *James J. Heckmann,* American Nobel laureate for Economics in the year 2000, who sees the cheapest measure by far in providing qualified early pedagogical offers, so as to integrate persons into society and qualify them for the employment market (DJI Bulletin 81 PLUS 1/2008, 1)

[73] For Rauschenbach (2007, 5), in recent years, the following has been introduced in a "family-political triple jump": each child's legal right to a place in a kindergarten (1996), the introduction of parenting money (2007), the agreed upon legal right of each child to a place in a child care facility as of the age of one (beginning in 2013).
Hans Rudolf Leu will speak at the **15th German Congress on Crime Prevention** on the topic of "Child day-care facilities' development and expansion. Quantitative and qualitative foundation for early childhood education"

Given the historical development of the public child day-care facilities in Germany, this was not necessarily to be expected.[74]

In Germany, ever since the year one, the care of one's own children was considered to be a *private matter*: hence, still at the end of the 1980s, which is not even two decades ago, in West Germany 99% of the children under the age of three and 88% of the three to six-year old children were cared for in their private environments when the mother was not working; in the event that she was working, the share of private caretaking did decrease, but it was still at 88% or 75% respectively.[75]

In the meantime the child day-care facilities as a place of upbringing is a lifeworld that is experienced by virtually all children in Germany – albeit very differently in scope and quality.[76] In 2002, in the Western federal states, except for the city states, the percentage of **children under the age of three years** in care outside the home was merely 2%; in the Eastern federal states it was 37% and in the city states it was 26%. In the year 2008 this percentage had increased to 12.2% in the Western states (including the city states) and in the Eastern states to 42.4%. Because, as of August 2013, owing to the Kinderfoerderungsgesetz (children fostering law)[77], children will have a legal right to a day-care place, the development of day-care accommodations for under three-year olds (still) has to be increased considerably." (DJI Thema 2009/2) This also applies against the background of the currently low number of hours per day in which children are looked after in the facilities: in the Western states, one third (33%) of the children are looked after outside of the family for a mere 5 hours per weekday; in the Eastern states this low caretaking time applied for fewer than half the children(16%); here 63% of the children are looked after for the whole day (more than 7 hours) (DJI Bulletin 81, 11).

The caretaking percentages for the **three to six-year old children were and are consi-derably higher**.[78] In the Eastern states anyhow, but also in the Western federal states, other than the city states, the number of available places corresponded to a caretaking quota of 69% in the year 1990, and this rose to a utilization quota of 91% in the year 2008. This expansion especially benefited children in the ages between three and four years: in 1992,

---

[74]   See in this regard, Rauschenbach 2009a, 138f.; also the Federal Ministry for Family, Seniors, Women and Youth (BMFSFJ)2005a, 37 and Sommerfeld 2007, 74.

[75]   In contrast, since the 1960s the child day-care facilities have been consistently expanded in der GDR, so that can speak about an "institutional" childhood in the East (Rauschenbach 2009a, 141).

[76]   In this regard also see the report issued by the Bertelsmann Foundation – "Country report on early child educational systems 2008" (Bock-Famulla 2008).

[77]   KiFöG – "Law on facilitation of children under three years of age in day care facilities and children day care centres" - in force since 1 January 2009; German government, federal states and local communities have agreed that, on average, until the year 2013 across Germany there would be a place in a child care facility for every third child under three years of age. One assumes that this will suffice to fulfil the legal claim for a place for children as of one year of age, which goes into force in 2013.

[78]   For this age group there has already been a legal claim to a kindergarten place since 1 January 1996.

31% of the three-year olds attended a kindergarten, in 2008 this figure was 81%; with the four and five-year olds the figure increased from 78% to 95% (Rauschenbach 2009, 142ff.)[79] However, in the Western federal states only 20% of the children utilized the offer of whole-day education, upbringing and caretaking; in the Eastern countries, by contrast, it was 63% (DJI Bulletin 81, 11); according to the expert commission for the *12ᵗʰ Child and Youth Report* (Federal Ministry for Family, Seniors, Women and Youth (BMFSFJ)2005a) an offer that fulfils the needs will only be attained when 50% of places available for child-care can be provided for full-day care. At the present time, though, parents' demand for full-day care for children under the age of three as well as for school children still lies far above the number of available places (Gragert and others 2008, 31).

All in all, the child day-care facilities have now become a **matter of course**: with regard to their expansion "one could notice a change in mindset in a breathtakingly short space of time.". It is "no longer a question of *whether*, but especially of *how* to expand the number of publicly offered child day-care facilities." (Rauschenbach 2009a, 145) According to the insights of neuroscientists and psychologists, an educational offer in the kindergarten both meets the educational needs of children as well as their need for education (Schneider 2009, 32).[80] However, as before, not all families, and thus not all children, make use of the non-compulsory offer of early education, upbringing and caretaking. Thus, for example, lower percentages of children with a migrational **background**[81] attend a child day-care fa-cility, and these children also only start later on, that is, fewer start before the age of three. Children under the age of three from families that draw **social security benefits** l likewise make less frequent use of this offer (DJI Bulletin 81, 11).[82]

---

[79] According to the findings of the *National Report on Education 2008*, in 2007 up to 95% of the 4 and 5 year-olds attended **child day-care facilities** – "although the utilization of the offer for child day-care facilities and child day-care is voluntary, it is increasingly becoming normal within the educational biography of children ... in the course hereof there still are significant regional differences with a view to the hours of care and the age in which children first make use of these offers" (BBE 2008, 50).

[80] Fundamentals on caretaking, on the effects on the development of the children, on the satisfaction of the parents, also see *Heitkötter* 2009. In 2004 the Conference of the state Education Ministers (KMK)/Youth Minister Conference adopted a framework for early education with the objective of not only providing education in primary school, but already making this obligatory in early childhood education. In the meantime all of the 16 federal states have elaborated education plans for the child day-care facilities, which are determined by the paradigm of equal footing and interdependency of upbringing, caretaking and education (Schneider 2009, 32).

[81] In the kindergartens of Western German, 29% of the children have a **migrational background**, but only 6% in Eastern Germany. Noticeable – and obviously more widespread than in the schools – is the unbalanced distribution of children with a migrational background in the facilities: more than 60% attend facilities in which an above-average number of children with migrational background are looked after – not a particularly favourable circumstance for the social integration of these children. "One can assume that these facilities with such a high share of children with migrational background need additional per-sonnel resources, if the high expectations placed on these facilities as places of integration for different cultures and early-lingual facilitation are to be met (BBE 2008, 53).
It goes without saying that the abilitiy to speak German properly is of considerable importance for the educational processes. Since 2005 the DJI-project "**Language Training in the Kindergarten**" has been working on supplying the corresponding materials for practical use in the field of preschool learning. In the meantime a tried-and-tested concept for integrated lingual groundwork has arisen (www.dji.de).

[82] Interesting, within this context, is the "atmospheric picture" gained in a study conducted by the German

Due to the demand for equal opportunities for all children[83] and the insight that the early educational processes in child day-care facilities play an important role that is not to be underestimated with regard to preparing children for school,[84] the question of whether it should be **compulsory** for children to attend a **kindergarten** as of the age of four or five, analogous to compulsory school education, is now under discussion.[85] This too is indicative of the change in mindset: "the public day-care facilities of the past, which used to be viewed as a fifth (emergency) tyre on the vehicle of early education of children, have now changed to an offer of early education for *all* children, without exception, because this is indispensable for their futures." (Rauschenbach 2009a, 145f.)

In the meantime, the *Bundesjugendkuratorium (Federal Youth Board)* even believes that the child day-care facilities are **overloaded with expectations**. The following is expected of them: they should activate educational reserves by means of early and targeted facilitation and support; provide an effective contribution to the creation of equal opportunities in the field of education; provide a contribution to an improved reconciliation of family and employment by providing a sufficient number of places

That are flexible with regard to the opening hours; compensate limitations and restraints in familial socialisation, for instance by giving children the opportunity of gaining group experiences or providing them with possibilities for activation that lie outside consumption of the media; improve societal integration, especially of people with a migrational background; take over tasks of a preventative social nature by means of early recognition of possible problematic constellations in the care and upbringing of some particular child. Certain requirements are associated with these expectations, which the facilities and the personnel working therein cannot comply with, given the currently applicable framework conditions. There is a "great **danger** that the child day-care facilities will fail, owing to requirements that are diffuse but complex at the same time."(2008, 10ff.)

Telekom Foundation (2010), which interviewed parents and non-parents on the importance of early childhood education, in particular with regard to their expectations pertaining to the role/function of the kindergarten/child day-care facilities.

[83] On the polarisation of life and educational opportunities of children and families and the challenges for child day-care facilities, also see Meier-Graewe 2009 (DJI Thema 2009/02) and the expert report for the 14th German Congress on Crime Prevention.

[84] Although the specific performance potential of the child day-care facilities should actually not be that of pre-emptive scholastic education, but rather a consistent individualisation of childlike learning (Rauschenbach 2009a,153; BJK 2008, 19ff.), the – as yet not solved – conflict between "individual facilitation" and "reaching a level of being ready for school" cannot be denied.

[85] The *Action Council for Education*, for instance, is in favour of mandatory kindergarten attendance, when it made the following recommendation to politics in its annual expert report in 2008: "As of the end of their second year, it is recommended that all children should be able to attend a kindergarten; this should be mandatory for children with a particular need for support; a mandatory preschool attendance as of the age of four years as well as an academic training of the preschool personnel so as to comply better with the educational mandate of the preschool field." (2008, 146).

At any rate, considerable **effort** will be required if the child day-care facilities should even remotely be placed in a position to meet the demands and expectations placed in them. These efforts include, in particular: the continued expansion of the child day-care facilities, especially for children under the age of three and this in particular in the Western federal states; the improvement of the personnel infrastructure, regarding the available personnel resources and the qualification of staff as well as the improvement of their professional image and status, whereas not only one quality offensive would be required, but – with the foreseeable lack of teachers trained for pre-school pupils – also an increase of educator training capacities.[86]

These efforts should also include the necessity of systematically and more strongly involving **parents** in the upbringing and educational processes of the child day-care facilities. Since, despite the "increase of publicly operated caretaking, education and upbringing, the comprehensive support and facilitation of children still remains a co-productive performance between the family, public care offerings and the broader social environment" (Heitkötter 2009, 21). Children day-care facilities should develop in the direction in which the consideration of families as contact groups should be expanded, moving toward becoming **centres for integrated and easily accessible service and support systems for** children and families (BJK 2008, 27; Stöbe-Blossey 2010, 95).

In this regard projects such as "Family Centres", "Children and Family Centres", "Parent-Child Centres" are being discussed and tested.

Examples of such centres are the British "Early Excellence Centres (EEC)", which were started in 1997 by the government, by means of a pilot programme. In the meantime there are more than 100 such centres. Their objective is to respond to the complex needs of families by providing offers coming from just one source. At the centre hereof is the involvement of the parents in the educational work and the children's development. By means of offers for further training and education the competences and confidence of parents are strengthened, so that they are better able to stand up for the interests of their children (Stöbe-Blossey 2010, 96).[87]

An approach to systematic implementation of such concepts over a large area has been pursued in the state of North Rhine-Westphalia in the form of **family centres** since early 2006. By 2012 one third of the roughly 9,000 child day-care facilities shall be expanded

---

[86] See in this regard DJI 2009a; DJI Bulletin 80, 2007; Bock-Famulla 2008; Komdat Jugendhilfe (Youth Welfare) Number 2/09 "Increasing the educator training capacities for teachers of pre-school children is necessary"; Heitkötter 2009 or also the article by Jeannette Otto in the ZEIT (weekly newspaper) No. 28 of 2 July 2009 "The child day care lie" or by Markus Wehner in the Frankfurter Allgemeinen Sonntagszeitung (weekly newspaper) No. 26 of 28 June 2009 "Too few goals, too little money – the expansion of child day-care is not progressing well".

[87] In Germany for instance, since 2000, the Heinz and Heide Dürr Foundation have been supporting the first Early Excellence Centre, with the pilot project "children and family centres – Schillerstraße", which is an establishment of the Pestalozzi-Fröbel-House, located in Berlin (www.early-excellence.de and the www.heinzundheideduerrstiftung.de.

to become such family centres, in which children and families are assisted jointly and sustainably supported. The objective is to merge education, upbringing and care as the task of child day-care facilities, with counselling offers and assistance for families. The development of children and the support of families can thus go hand in hand.[88]

3.2.2
Child day-care facilities as place of prevention of violence

As the first publicly organised and operated instance outside of the family, the child day-care facilities also represent a place for the prevention of violence, and this is particularly valid for the day-care centres: they can offer both children and families "encouragement, assistance and support at a very early stage and have the effect of potential protective factors against the inclination to use violence." (Sommerfeld 2007, 82)[89]

However, the reason for this is not the violence between the children or toward the caretaking persons in the child day-care centre itself: although, since the 1990s "violence in kindergartens" has been an issue for specialists and also for the media ("monster kids" and "kindergarten rambos"),[90] there is not really a "violence" problem in the child day-care centres (Sommerfeld 2007, 82).

At least there is hardly any data on this: in the police crime statistics this is not disclosed – in total, for the entire country, in 2007 there were only 83 children under the age of six who were registered for accounts of bodily harm – and according to the information of the Statutory Accident Insurance in the year 2004 there were 3.4 so-called "scuffling-accidents" per every 1.000 children in day-care facilities, of which two thirds occurred with children as of age 5 or older. The figures have stagnated since they were first recorded in 1990.[91]

Besides, using the "violence phrase" for child behaviour is problematic at any rate and also not appropriate, in particular for children of preschool age: "bodily conflict resolutions are appropriate within the preschool age bracket and in respect to child development, ... "Violence" is a "container" phrase for a broad range of socially undesired and yet age-typical behaviour right up to destructive behavioural patterns,

---

[88]   Quoted from the internet entry "Family Centre NRW" www.familienzentrum.nrw.de); in this regard also see the presentation by Stoebe-Blossey 2010, 95ff

[89]   This order has already resulted from the KJHG: day-care facilities for children have the public mandate of fostering and supporting every child in his/her development toward an independent and socially-adapted personality and to counter (the development of) disadvantages

[90]   In this regard also see the documentation of a hearing of the Bundesjugendkuratoriums (State Youth Board of Trustees) 1998 on the "Mythos of the Monsterkids" (Arbeitsstelle Kinder- und Jugendkriminalitätsprävention 1999).

[91]   Information by Sommerfeld 2007, 78. While the statistics of the German Statutory Accident Insurance (DGUV) on the school children accidents of 2008 are available and differentiate between the types of child day-care facilities, they do not differentiate between "scuffling accidents" and other incidents (www.dguv.de).

which hardly can be dealt with appropriately within normal facilities." (Sommerfeld 2007, 77f.).[92]

Hence, **prevention** within the "child day-care facilities as place of education" rather has a **universal** alignment. Its primary objective is to foster social competences, to prevent or reduce disadvantages, and to promote the integration and social participation of children – and thus also to oppose the appearance of societal disintegration and precarious life circumstances, which emerge in the everyday life of child day-care facilities as the increase of childlike behavioural patterns and parental upbringing difficulties and which might cause the caretakers considerable problems.

The approaches aimed at prevention are as manifold and heterogeneous as the supporting structure of the child day-care facilities with their variety of institutional forms and pedagogical concepts. Traditionally, the field of action is characterised by projects of individual facilities or sponsors at local or regional levels. The clientele is not only the children within the day-care facilities themselves, but also their parents and the skilled personnel (see Sommerfeld 2007, 84ff.on this and the following).

Apart from situative interventions – for instance in handling conflicts or facilitating participation – the pedagogical staff also initiates offers and projects. Since child educational processes are always also characterised by the child's independent interaction with its own environment in which children actively have to get to know their surroundings, every child thus becomes an actor and co-producer in the course of its education (Rauschenbach 2009a, 154). It's not about "teaching" children something, but about perceiving and following up the themes of the children in dialogue with them by observing their playing and interaction processes (Sommerfeld 2007, 86).

In this regard, **themes** are, for instance, the strengthening of the self-esteem of children, also and especially with regard to dealing with **differences**: in the day-care facility each child's family culture, gained from its parents and family, comes into contact with a variety of different cultures – not only pertaining to the ethnic background, but also regarding the greatly varying life-concepts and familial life circumstances. Broadly speaking, for the professional staff, intercultural competence is becoming a factor of decisive importance as they increasingly find themselves in an highly heterogeneous, socio-economic but also ethnically-culturally divided society, which is drifting further and further apart.[93]

---

[92]   In this regard also see the remarks in the expert report on the focal topic of the 12th German Congress on Crime Prevention "Violence as a learning opportunity: on the necessity and benefits of age-appropriate understanding of violence" (Steffen 2008, 255ff.).

[93]   Regarding the concept of intercultural competence, see, for example, the theses paper of the Bertelsmann Foundation (2006).

In the meantime there are standardised curricula of social training programmes for kindergarten children that are focussed on the improvement of social competences – thus, making friends, resolving social conflicts, recognising and regulating emotions[94] are available in standardised curriculum form. They are intended for a fairly long timeframe and focus on the entire kindergarten group – universal prevention – not merely on individual "difficult" children, and are conducted by pedagogically skilled staff. For this, as for other prevention programmes, the qualification of the staff is of key importance.

This is the case in particular for strategies aimed at **selective and indicated prevention of violence**, which are then used if child day-care centres, as described in above, are to perform preventative work within social **early warning systems** and be placed in a position to recognise possibly problematic constellations in the care and upbringing of a child as soon as possible. Given the current structural conditions, the educators neither have the requisite leeway nor the required additional training: "The work with families that are in particular problem situations requires a degree of professionalism that cannot be assumed to be present either on the part of heads of staff or the teaching staff." (Sommerfeld 2007, 98f.)

3.3
School as a place of education and prevention

"Increasingly, scholastic success is regarded as a relevant factor in the distribution of societal opportunities and risks."[95]

3.3.1
School as a place of education

Although education is more than school and leading a successful life is built on social integration as well as on educational processes within families, as well as establishments of the Child and Youth Welfare and vocational training, school is without a doubt "the central public place of educations for children and adolescents in the process of growing up" (Rauschenbach 2009a, 166). Education in school age plays a key role for individual development, both for social participation and for conveying competences (BBE 2008, 61).[96]

Not least because of this significance, school at the same time is a severely criticised place of education: "School pupils speak about their fears of school and their aversion to attending school; parents and parents' representatives mention reservations

---

[94] For instance www.papilio.de, (in this regard also Scheithauer/Mayer 2008 and 2009) or www.faustlos. de; both programmes for prevention of violence have been evaluated. According to the findings by *Beelmann* (2009, 261) the social training programmes for children, however, show less impact than the training programmes for parents.

[95] DJI Bulletin 81, 1/2008, 11.

[96] The central role of school also is expressed in the compulsory school attendance.

and criticism pertaining to school. Employers complain about the education levels of a considerable number of adolescents that are (too) low, calling it a problem of education and training. Virtually ten percent of adolescents leave school without a qualifying degree. Scholastic performance studies such as PISA, TIMMS and IGLU[97] confirm that the German school system does less than schools in many other countries and, in particular, it does not even out differences owing to the social and migrational background of school pupils, but rather reinforces them." (BJK 2004b, 5)[98]

Hence it appears that the German school system does not render the **educational performance that is and ought to be expected of it** – for instance in view of the constitutional right to equal opportunity in education or in view of the right to a comprehensive general school education that is proclaimed, for example, in school curricula.[99]

In international comparison, with regard to the right to **equal opportunities, it** was the PISA-studies in particular that pointed out the significant disadvantages of children and adolescents with a socially weaker background. Gaining access to higher education and high-school graduation remains a central barrier for adolescents from families of the lower social classes. A consequence of a higher socio-economic status is a high-school quota that is up to five times higher and a secondary general school quota that is up to three times lower.

Risk situations lead to a significant deterioration of educational opportunities – and these risk situations have increased in recent years: In 2006, more than every tenth child under the age of 18 years lived in a family in Germany in which no parent was working. 13% of the children grew up in families in which nobody had a qualification of the secondary stage I. With 23% of the children, the family's income was below the "risk of poverty" line. 4.2 million, or 28%, of the children are affected by at least one of these risk situations.

Migrational background is a "risk situation" that leads to disadvantages in all levels of the school system – and in some regions young people with migrational background represent a share of more than half of their age group. More than 40% of the

---

[97] See above FN 19.

[98] Whereby there is no such thing as a *German* school: cultural sovereignty, which includes responsibility for all public schools, lies solely with the federal states and, in accordance with the federalistic structures, the design of the German school systems is highly heterogeneous and multi-faceted. The question of what the right school structure is has been a matter of controversy for many years. Presently, once again, there is heated discussion of questions such as the duration of primary school, whether or not to have independent secondary modern schools, and who has the final say regarding whether a given pupil may enter academic high school, etc. In this regard see, for example, the article "Auf neuen Bildungswegen" (On new educational paths) in the Sueddeutsche Zeitung (newspaper) of 19 January 2010 or also the verbal dispute "We need a new culture of learning" by the Culture Ministers of Bavaria, Hamburg and Saxony in the Sueddeutsche Zeitung of 10 March 2010.

[99] See in this regard and in the following the Federal Ministry for Family, Seniors, Women and Youth (BMFSFJ) 2005a, 280ff., BBE 2008, 10ff., Action Council for Education 2007, 135ff.

adolescents of both immigrant generations but only 14% of the adolescents without migrational background belong to the so-called risk group with low reading competence. Even with the same social status, school pupils with a migrational background less frequently attend an academic high school (college preparatory school), are more frequently to be found in the types of schools offering a lower level of qualification, leave schools of general education (secondary school) twice as often as native German school pupils without having obtained at least a secondary modern school qualification and have delayed and less successful transitions into vocational training[100] (there are no such disadvantages after vocational training, once this has been reached and successfully concluded).

What can be noticed, however, is the reversal of **gender specific disadvantages** of girls: girls and young women are becoming increasingly more successful; in contrast, new problematic situations are to be found with boys. The risk of boys and young men failing in the educational system is increasing. This is particularly the case for those with a migrational background. Boys also more frequently repeat a school year.[101]

All in all, the German school system produces too many **educational losers**: "repeaters", children who refuse to go to school and dropout pupils. According to the PISA-study 2003, almost one quarter (23%) of all fifteen-year olds had repeated at least one school year in the course of their time at school.[102] The number of children who refuse to go to school – those who do not attend for more than ten school days per half-year – is estimated at 300,000. In addition, there are the so-called "truants". This is particularly prevalent at secondary general schools and schools for children with learning difficulties.[103] The number of dropouts – school students leaving school without a secondary general certificate – is decreasing somewhat throughout Germany, however, in 2008 it still was at a level of 7% (or 64,400 adolescents).[104]

According to the results of the international **performance studies,** the German school system obviously does not succeed sufficiently at imparting a basic training or educational minimum in language, mathematics and scientific competences for all school

---

[100] **Joerg Dittmann, Sandra Heisig and Jan Goebel** will speak at the **15ᵗʰ German Congress on Crime Prevention** on the topic of "Prevention Strategies at the Transition from School to Vocational Training – Approaches in the Work with Disadvantaged Adolescents".

[101] **Klaus Hurrelmann** will speak at the **15ᵗʰ German Congress on Crime Prevention** on the topic of "Competence Deficits of Young Men – a Challenge for Preventative Work".

[102] A study conducted on behalf of the Bertelsmann Foundation, on the costs for repeating a school year in Germany ascertained the following: "Repeat years – expensive and ineffective". Repeat years for pupils who had not been promoted, neither led to an improvement of their cognitive development, nor did the pupils who remained in the original class benefit from this instrument. With striking differences regarding the types of schools and state-dependent differences regarding the repeater quota, each and every year more than 931 million euros are spent for repeating a class in Germany (Klemm 2009).

[103] SPIEGEL interview of 7 October 2009 with Karlheinz Thimm "One has to fight for difficult pupils"

[104] SPIEGELONLINE report of 11 November 2009.

pupils. In a longitudinal cut, improvements in performance have been established, however, according to the PISA studies, approximately one quarter of the 15 year-olds has to be considered a risk group, as, owing to clear lacks in reading competence and in dealing with mathematical procedures and models, they might have significant problems with commencing vocational training. Particularly strongly represented among these risk school pupils are adolescents from workers' families as well as from families with a migrational background (Federal Ministry for Family, Seniors, Women and Youth (BMFSFJ)2005a, 282).[105]

This confirms the aforementioned supposition that the German school system does not render the educational performance that it should and that is expected of it. However – this has already been pointed out – the high degree of social selectivity of the German educational system, the particular disadvantages for children from the poorly educated social classes in which education is not considered as being so important, or for children of people with a migrational background, cannot only be blamed on the schools. Obviously, the other upstream or supplementary places of education such as "family", "child day-care" and "offerings by the Child and Youth Welfare" are not (any longer) or not (yet) sufficiently able to render the educational performance for adolescents that is required for their educational success at school.[106]

In this regard the family plays a key role. Inability of the family to fulfil their duties with regard to care-taking and support, upbringing and education, results in disadvantages for the children which subsequently can only be evened out with a lot of effort. Early help and early facilitation, supplementing private family care with public caretaking offers could even out such disadvantages and promote educational justice. "School is a joint responsibility of teachers, parents and, moreover, the pupils themselves. We must focus on drawing parents' attention to their responsibilities for their children." (Lenzen 2009, 9)[107]

---

[105] An additional indicator for the weaknesses of the German school system is the frequency of private coaching: "Teaching and learning outside of school is a part of everyday life for families in Germany" (Federal Ministry for Family, Seniors, Women and Youth (BMFSFJ) 2005a, 283). A study conducted on behalf of the Bertelsmann Foundation on "Expenses for **Private Coaching** – Expensive and Unfair Equalisation for Lack of Individual Attention" concluded that the high degree of private coaching in Germany is not only indicative of a lack in the educational system, but is, above all, also unjust, as not everyone can afford it. This worsens the equal opportunities of the educational system (Klemm/Klemm 2010).

[106] *Lenzen* (2009, 7) on this finding: "From a national economy point of view, one can also say: this part of the upcoming generation is being systematically held back from the national economy." The Stanford Professor Eric H. Hanushek, the Munich educational economist Professor Ludger Wößmann and the international PISA-coordinator Andreas Schleicher have conducted the study "The High Cost of Low Educational Performance" for the OECD, which also conducts the PISA studies,. According to their calculations, earnings in Germany would be correspond to five times that of the entire annual economic performance or an additional annual growth rate of 0.8%, if the children in German schools could be brought up to the level of the children in Finnish schools (www.zeit.de/gesellschaft/schule/201001/oecd-educationsausgaben? page=all&print vom 21.1.2010)

[107] **Liv Berit Koch and Maria Macher** will speak at the **15th German Congress on Crime Prevention** on the topic of "District Mothers in Berlin-Neukoelln – Presentation of the Project and First Evaluation Results".

At any rate, the problems of social, cultural and also education-related segregation represent a central challenge for educational policy. An answer for this challenge – "the central hope of educational policy per se" – is the nationwide establishment and expansion of **all-day schools**.[108]

With a share of only 5% of all schools in Germany, all-day schools have been an exception[109] and, for a long time, they were a taboo topic in Western Germany and regarded there as a massive assault on the family and the parents' rights to bring up their own children.

In the meantime this image has changed. For some years now, all-day schools have come to be viewed as a contemporary reply to the changing needs of parents, which require finding ways in which to reconcile work with the upbringing of children, reacting to new demands and expectations regarding the children's education and enabling a better facilitation, in particular for children and adolescents who have an educational disadvantage (Federal Ministry for Family, Seniors, Women and Youth (BMFSFJ) 2005a, 305f.) – the analogy to the development and evaluation of the child day-care facilities is impossible to overlook.

An important impetus for the expansion of all-day schools has been provided with the investment programme **"Zukunft Bildung und Betreuung" (Future Education and Care)** (IZBB), which is presumably the largest education-political reform programme currently being carried out. With this programme, the Federal Government, which has no competence of its own in cultural and educational policy), supports the federal states' demand-oriented build up and expansion of all-day schools.[110] All decisions on which schools and types of schools are to be supported, as well as the contentual and staffing arrangements for these schools, fall within the competence of the federal states. According to the annual reports of the federal states, a total of 7,129 schools were supported or scheduled for facilitation between 2003 and 2009. The all-day school programme is accompanied and evaluated scientifically.[111]

Establishment of all-day schools in Germany will not only provide the opportunity to expand the number of hours of the conventional teaching schools and traditional half-day schools, but also to supplement them with **other educational contents and forms of learning** (Rauschenbach 2009a, 177).[112] The debate concerning the all-day

---

[108]   Rauschenbach (2009a, 177), who sees all-day schools as a chance for the future.

[109]   Internationally, Germany is virtually the only country that allows itself the luxury of a half-day school; according to current data by the Ministry of Education and Arts, the half-day model is still valid for approximately two thirds of all school administration units (Stecher u.a. 2009).

[110]   On 12 May 2003, the administrative agreement to this investment programme was jointly signed by the Federal and State governments. A total of four billion euros were provided for the years 2003 to 2007, and these funds can still be spent until the end of 2009 (www.bmbf.de/de/3735.php)

[111]   At the centre of this is the "Study on Development of All-Day Schools" (StEG) under the direction of a consortium (www.projektsteg.de); in this regard also see Stecher and others 2009.

[112]   **Christian Pfeiffer** will speak at the **15th German Congress on Crime Prevention** on the topic of "Dai-

school has also once again stimulated the discussion about an **opening** of the school toward a lifeworld and about the **networking** of the school with other pedagogical institutions, in particular from the field of **Youth Welfare** – to utilize the chance of combining the strengths of the school with the strengths of the other educational players (BMFSFJ 2005a, 282). For the afternoon programmes can be provided by outside sponsors[113] – and here "the Child and Youth Welfare will assume a prominent position" (Federal Ministry for Family, Seniors, Women and Youth (BMFSFJ) 2005a, 306).

However, it still has not been clarified whether and how this "prominent position" should actually be occupied; how school and Child and Youth Welfare can cooperate. For "in view of its own decidedly anti-school tradition, in the horizon of its consistent participation-oriented self-image in dealing with the children and adolescents" (Rauschenbach 2008, 7), the **Child and Youth Work** still has a hard time in getting along with the topic of education.[114]

At any rate, the *Bundesjugendkuratorium (Federal Youth Board)* is pursuing the discussion about the establishment of all-day schools and the attempts of Child and Youth Welfare to assert themselves as partners of schools "with scepticism" (2004b, 9).[115] From the perspective of the Bundesjugendkuratorium (Federal Youth Board of Trustees) **new places of education** are required as "places of public responsibility" and a new overall concept of all-day education, behind which "a supporting alliance of all institutions involved in matters concerning education and upbringing must stand" (2004b, 17)[116] – and a new understanding of education, for which Child and Youth Welfare can provide "an indispensable contribution" (2004b, 20). Namely: "to promote a different kind of education that is actually centred around the children and takes them seriously as subjects of their educational process" (2004b, 20). [117]

---

ly fitness training at school. The way toward better performance at school and less violence –concept for a pilot trial"

[113] School and external sponsors must reach an agreement on a joint concept; the school administration has the overall responsibility.

[114] On the educational performance of child and youth work, the area of Child and Youth Welfare, which is the first candidate for cooperation with the schools – to convey social and personal competences – and the typical "learning settings" for this – such as the non-compulsory nature of participation, view of the whole person, topicality and reality-reference of the learning experience – see the remarks in the 12th Child and Youth Report (Federal Ministry for Family, Seniors, Women and Youth (BMFSFJ) 2005a, 303).
Vera Bethge, Irina Neander and Marita Stolt will speak at the **15th German Congress on Crime Prevention** on the topic of "Joint Responsibility for Education and Upbringing – School and Youth Welfare in Cooperation".

[115] Although, fundamentally, the *Bundesjugendkuratorium (Federal Youth Board)* has a very positive view of all-day schools: they offer all participants a great variety of options, bring school learning and extracurricular forms of educational and rearing processes together, enable the involvement of social-cultural and athletic organisations and as such offer the foundation and time for intensive facilitation of individual talents (2003, II.)

[116] An understanding that is only based on cooperation is not enough (BJK 2003 IV.)

[117] Owing to their value orientation and participative structures, Youth Welfare and youth work "are particularly qualified to commit themselves to an understanding of a new integrative education that is oriented

So that changes within the meaning of forward looking concepts are actually accepted at the schools, and so that cooperations arise there structurally and not just sporadically, the *Bundesjugendkuratorium (Federal Youth Board)* considers that it is "urgently necessary *that comprehensive concepts for education and upbringing are developed on location, and that these can be brought together and bundled by **local alliances for education*** and further developed both conceptually and in respect to contents." (BJK 2004b, 6f.)

This objective – or rather vision – is described as follows by the *12th Child and Youth Report*: "The interplay of various education players and matters is to be developed socio-spatially and organised in municipal responsibility. The objective is to build up a municipal educational landscape as an infrastructure for children and adolescents which is supported by services and facilities of the school, Child and Youth Welfare, cultural facilities, clubs and associations, institutions for the promotion of health, as well as private and business players on location" (Federal Ministry for Family, Seniors, Women and Youth (BMFSFJ) 2005a, 351).

Given that high objectives and expectations are connected with all-day schools and that these go far beyond a school reform and as such are correspondingly difficult to realise owing to the fact that this is a matter of creating all-day public educational, care and upbringing offerings for children and adolescents of school age with the involvement of several players, in particular players from Child and Youth Welfare, then this complex of problems will apply to a much greater extent with regard to the development of **municipal educational landscapes**.

The "**Learning On-Location**" **programme** which is a joint initiative of the Federal Ministry for Education and Research and German Foundations, is the attempt at creating such educational landscapes that was begun in 2008. This programme, which runs through 2012, promotes the build-up of a model local education management (system) in 40 selected county towns and independent cities for an improved interlocking of existing offers and institutions. Municipal education management should enable inter-agency control with the involvement of all educational players and include civic commitment. The objective is that the municipalities will develop into excellent educational locations, in which citizens can go through a successful educational biography in a convincing and clear educational system, starting in early childhood and continuing through adult education.[118]

---

to justice, solidarity and participation." (2004b, 20)

[118] Learning On Location" is a central component of the Federal Government's "Advancement through Education" qualification initiative; see the BMBF 2009 a and b; coalition agreement 2009, 59. **Siegfried Haller** will speak at the **15th German Congress on Crime Prevention** on the topic of "Project of the BMBF – "Learning On Location – an Approach to Prevention".

3.3.2
School as a place of prevention of violence

The demand that schools, as places of public education, should also do something about violence and the propensity of children and adolescents to use violence, is not new.[119] Hence, particularly for the first half of the 1990s, there was a veritable "boom" in research and prevention on the topic of "violence at schools", which, however, abated in the second half of the decade. In the meantime, however, the debate has become clearly more objective, but always flares up again every time there are spectacular acts of violence at schools (in this regard, on the occasion of the "**rampages**" of Winnenden or Ansbach 2009).[120]

It is especially these and similar isolated cases of spectacular acts of violence, which attract enormous medial as well as political attention, that contribute to the view that violence by school pupils at the crime scene "school" is on the rise.[121] However, this is a perception that is not in agreement with the existent empirical findings: an increase in physical violence at schools cannot be backed up by criminal or other statistical data or by repeatedly conducted surveys designed to expose undetected, unreported crime.[122]

Insofar as the **police criminal statistics** of the federal states allow for the corresponding analyses – such analyses are not possible at the Federal Statistics level – the data regularly shows that only a small portion of the acts of violence committed by adolescents (and also other offences) transpire at school; that these criminal offences have hardly, if at all, increased in recent years – and that such increases have definitely not been "dramatic". Rather, the progression of these statistics is "wave-like" over time: that is, the numbers go up a bit and then they come back down.

The relatively insignificant importance of the crime scene "school" for the scope and development of juvenile violence is all the more remarkable because children and adolescents spend a large part – the largest part – of the day there.

---

[119] See also *Schubarth* 2010, 9ff., 57ff., whose book "Gewalt und Mobbing an Schulen" (Violence and Mobbing at schools) is well worth reading and provides a factual and empirically based overview regarding the dimensions, various forms and causes of violence and mobbing at schools, as well as the possibilities of prevention and intervention.

[120] "**Rampages**" at German schools are extremely rare isolated cases; there are no clusters or series in the data. As far as can be judged, the perpetrators also do not fit into the usual pattern of juvenile violence, as they previously were outwardly inconspicuous and not considered as having a tendency toward violence – and therefore do not provide any occasion for preventing violence. The recently published book by *Britta Bannenberg* (2010) on rampages, the recognition of warning signals and the prevention options is highly recommended.
Herbert Scheithauer will speak at the **15th German Congress on Crime Prevention** on the topic of "Dealing with the Leaking and Threats to use Serious Forms of Violence at German schools. The Berlin Leaking-Project and NETWASS".

[121] The significance of the media for the public thematisation and perception of "juvenile violence" was presented in detail in the expert report on the main topic of the 12th German Congress on Crime Prevention (Steffen 2008); also see Schubarth 2010, 9ff.

[122] See also explanations in Steffen 2008, 249ff.

These findings are regularly objected to on the grounds that there is more violence and in particular more brutality at schools, but the schools do not report it for fear of damaging their "image". This may apply in individual cases – although certainly not in cases of such brutal violence. However, that this is not the rule in general is backed up by the results of repeatedly conducted surveys as well as analyses by the German Statutory Accident Insurance Company on scuffling accidents at schools, which are insured.

Thus, surveys conducted in 1994, 1999 and 2004, with the same survey instruments, with representatively selected school pupils of Bavarian schools in the 5th to 13th grades, show that there was no increase in physical violence during this period. On the contrary: physical violence between school pupils and against physical objects also decreased – marginally by 1999, significantly by 2004 – as was the case with psychological violence; verbal aggression was however stated as being more frequent. There were no indications that the "violence situation at schools" might have gotten worse in general.[123]

In 2004, a survey that was conducted with school pupils of all grades in the state of Mecklenburg-Western Pomerania and was comparable to a survey conducted there in 1997 showed a significant decrease in violence. The remarkable thing was a considerable increase in the willingness of the school pupils and teachers alike to report such incidents to the police.[124]

Another analysis, coming from a different approach and thus of particular interest, confirms these empirical findings: the analysis of the German Statutory Accident Insurance company (DGUV). As it is relatively unlikely that schools would not report damages covered by insurance, this data may be assumed to be quite reliable. According to current statistics of the accident insurers – they insure school pupils against accidents happening during school attendance and on the way to and from school – the frequency of so-called **scuffling accidents decreased by approximately one quarter between** 2000 and 2007. Statistically seen, every tenth accident at schools providing a general education is due to an act of violence. Annually, one out of every hundred school pupils has to receive medical treatment after a skirmish.

In one out of every 7,000 cases (the rate was slightly less), an act of violence resulted in a fractured bone.[125]

---

[123] Fuchs and others 2005

[124] State criminal police Mecklenburg-Western Pomerania /Bornewasser 2004.

[125] The insurance companies for school children's accident insurance receive reports on scuffling accidents that necessitate a visit to a doctor. Cases in which this was not necessary, as well as forms of psychological violence, such as chaffing, bullying, mobbing are not recorded for statistical purposes. In 2008 there were a total of 1.3 million reportable school accidents – 78/1000 school pupils – and 118.000 reportable accidents on the way to or from school – 6.9/1000 school pupils (www.dguv.de).
According to an earlier analysis, the number of reportable cases resulting from "scuffling accidents" decreased from 1993 to 1995, then increased until 1998 and has since then been decreasing continually. This applies to all types of schools, whereby the secondary modern school has proven to be the school with the greatest amount of violence. The percentage of reported scuffling accidents that entailed frac-

Contrary to the perception of "increased violence at schools", all empirical findings show that there has been no general increase in physical violence and/or brutality in the past few years. On the contrary: despite increased sensitisation toward school violence and an increased willingness to report incidents to the police, the figures on incidents are tending to go down.

If, despite this, school is one of the central places for the **prevention of violence**[126], then not because it is the venue at which particularly many and/or severe acts of violence transpire, but rather because school – analogous to the child day-care centres – is the one place at which children and adolescents reliably spend time and are therefore accessible in principle for preventive measures and programmes.[127]

Hence, strategies for the prevention of violence at school are targeted on the one hand at preventing or reducing violence that can occur between school pupils at or on the way to or from school and, on the other hand, at positively influencing children's and adolescents' actual use of or readiness to use violence. After all, within the context of its upbringing and educational responsibility, school has "the social mandate of safeguarding the personal integrity and dignity of each and every school pupil. Owing to its status as a public educational facility, each school is obliged in principle to fulfil this responsibility with the appropriate pedagogical professionality and competence." (Schubarth 2010, 101)

Moreover, school is also a central place for the prevention of violence because school itself is involved in the "production" of violence and can exert an influence on the development of violence through appropriate organisation of the school and learning culture (Melzer 2004; Schubarth 2010, 51).[128]

Albeit only to a certain point: violent behaviour with "school" being the reason is dependent on a multitude of factors that can only be influenced by the school to a certain extent, if at all. School-related framework conditions such as the school buildings or the size of the class can be changed, albeit not easily. The same applies for the framework set by the school system: compulsory education, grading pressure, the division into different types of schools. Then there are the changed conditions for growing up

---

tures went down too. Thus an increase in brutality cannot be established on the basis of this data either (Federal Association of Accident insurers 2005).

[126]   On strategies for the prevention of violence at schools also see Hanke 2007.

[127]   All prevention programmes targeted at the class use this option; some of them focus on the non-compulsory nature of participation, whereby violence preventative learning can presumably be intensified (Hanke 2007, 119).

[128]   See also Melzer, who points out the many correlations between violent behaviour of school pupils and school culture variables, but also the difficulties of interpreting a causation link from such correlations (2004, 40).
    Siegfried Arnz will be speaking at the **15th German Congress on Crime Prevention** on the topic of "New chances for successful prevention by reforming the school structure".

and the social behaviour brought along by the children, the lack of perspective with regard to availability of vocational training or subsequent job opportunities or also the living and integrational conditions of school pupils with a migrational background (Hanke 2007, 106).

Hence, strategies for the prevention of violence at schools are targeted at various players and groups, as follows:[129] at the **school administration** – ministries for culture and education, academic supervisory officers, heads of school, all of whom create the structural framework for the prevention of violence at school; at the **school** as a whole, for instance by means of strategies aimed at the qualification of the staff for violence prevention in upbringing and educational work[130]; at the **school pupils,** for instance the numerous conflict mediator programmes (peer mediation)[131]; at programmes against mobbing[132] or also curricular programmes[133], of which however, as far as is evident, none have been developed in coproduction together with the respective school; at the **parents**, who are however frequently only integrated into the violence prevention work once a corresponding problem is already at hand; at the **public**, not least with the purpose of cultivating the school's image per se[134]; at players **outside of the school**, who have designed and developed virtually all of the concepts or programmes that are applied in the school; and at the training and further education of **teachers**.

Presently, the **central strategy** is to be found in the **further education** of teachers, in order to strengthen the prevention of violence at schools at the different levels of action. Further education tries to compensate for that which did not find sufficient

---

[129] See on the following Hanke 2007, 112ff.; a short overview on prevention programmes for the school can be found at Melzer 2004, 45. On the "multi-modal prevention of violence with children and adolescents" Lösel 2004 An informative, comprehensive overview of school prevention and intervention programmes is provided by Schubarth 2010, 113ff.
    Hartmut Pfeiffer and Peter Wetzels will be speaking at the **15th German Congress on Crime Prevention** on the topic of ",PaC - Prevention als Chance' - Implementation and Evaluation of an integrated Programme of Municipal Crime Prevention".
    Ria Uhle will be speaking at the **15th German Congress on Crime Prevention** on the topic of "Change, Upheavals, Crises - Prevention of Violence at Schools undergoing Change"

[130] An example for this is the Constance training model (KTM); Information on this, e.g. to be found at www.friedenspaedagogik.de. The "Abseits?!" media package (off-sides) was developed by the police crime prevention of the federal and state governments and then placed at the schools' disposal. The purpose: making recommendations to the teachers for their work in the classrooms on six topics pertaining to the prevention of violence.

[131] This also includes the "mediate" programme developed by the WEISSER RING; additional information on the programmes at www.bmev.de (Federal Association Mediation e.V.) and www.mediation-partizipation.de.

[132] Probably the best-known of these programmes, which has successfully been deployed for years already in numerous countries, is the anti-bullying-intervention programme according to Olweus (Schubarth 2010, 142ff. and www.clemson.edo/olweus/.

[133] For instance "Faustlos", www.faustlos.de. (without fists)

[134] Prominent example: the Rüthli-school in Berlin. **Cordula Heckmann** will be speaking at the **15th German Congress on Crime Prevention** on the topic of "Campus Rüthli CR2 – from a school with a dubious reputation to a pilot project".

consideration in the course of regular training;[135] to provide teachers with the basic qualification that can place them in a position of, apart from the educational responsibility, also meeting their not less important upbringing responsibility. Currently at least, functional prevention of violence at schools significantly depends on the personal, rather coincidental commitment of the responsible persons, especially in the field of school administration. (Hanke 2007, 125f.)

Apart from these programmes and measures which, within the meaning of selective crime convention, directly or indirectly have the objective of preventing or decreasing violence in childhood and adolescence, schools also apply **generally supportive measures** of universal prevention, which can have a violence prevention effect, but do not have this as their primary objective and hence cannot be described here as violence preventative strategies.[136] Such prevention programmes, which are not specific to violence, promote, for example, social and communicative competences, moral development, dealings with the media, intercultural learning, or democracy and human rights education.[137]

With regard to the **effectiveness** of prevention and intervention programmes *Schubarth* (2010, 183) sums up as follows: to date, of the numerous programmes and measures in **Germany,** only a part has been scientifically evaluated. Thereby, predominantly positive results were attained. However, for the most part, the evaluations pertained to the introduction or pilot phase – little is known about the long-term effects – and in part were conducted by the authors themselves.

On average, the **international evaluation findings** display positive effects, especially dependent on the age of the children, their risk burdens, the quality of implementation, and the integration of the measures within the school context. However, evaluation findings cannot be transferred, say from the USA to Germany, without further work.

All in all one can establish that the prevention of violence and the facilitation of social competences are ongoing tasks of school education and upbringing and closely linked to **scholastic development** (Schubarth 2010, 189 ff; similar Melzer 2004, 46 and Melzer/Schubarth/Ehninger 2004). While scholastic development cannot be equated with successful prevention of violence, prevention of violence and mobbing are particularly promising if they are implemented in a multistage school development process. Successful violence preventative programmes and activities can thus also activate scholastic development programmes, which then in turn create positive conditions for anchoring violence preventative measures (Hanke 2007, 128; Melzer/Schubarth/Ehninger 2004, 255ff.).

---

[135] Because: "Teacher training probably displays the most sluggish reaction to the prevention of violence in the area of school" (Hanke 2007,123).

[136] On understanding prevention of violence, see the remarks in chapter 2.2.

[137] **Harald Weilnböck** will be speaking at the **15th German Congress on Crime Prevention** on the topic of "Education in Times of Extremism".

And another point that has to be noted: the striking finding that virtually without exception the empirical studies on "violence at school", only examine violence committed by school pupils and only develop and use prevention programmes and measures directed against this violence. The **violence of teachers** toward school pupils and the **prevention** thereof is a topic much less frequently, if at all. However, there is evidence that such psychological, physical and also sexual violence have occurred and do occur; however there are no proven empirical findings on the scope and forms of this violence.

The best source for this would be representative school children surveys, but in the studies conducted in recent years, as far as is apparent, the topic of "teacher violence" has not been broached. The reasons for this, according to study commissioned by the European Union 2001 on "Measures against Violence at Schools: a Report from Germany" is that investigations of teacher violence against scholars are hardly possible here, since the officials that have to authorise such investigations are at the same time the highest superiors of the teachers.[138]

In the German speaking area, *Volker Krumm* (University of Salzburg) appears to be the only person who has frequently grappled empirically with the topic of teacher violence. Thus, for instance, within the framework of the Austrian part of the TIMMS-investigation in 1995, a representative random group of approx 10,000 school pupils from all kinds of schools of the 7th and 8th grades as well as the graduating classes of the 10th, 11th or 12th grade of the various secondary schools were surveyed as to which extent they were victims of violence by school pupils and teachers (treated unfairly? Feelings hurt? Galled in any other way?), or had observed this. "The prevalence investigation showed: ,violence' (,mobbing') of teachers against school pupils is just as common as ,violence' of pupils against pupils" (Krumm and others 1997). In a further investigation (in 1997?) in Austria, Germany and Switzerland, almost 3000 students were surveyed as to whether they had experienced hurtful behaviour by teachers in the course of their schooldays. 78% answered this question in the affirmative (Krumm/Weiß 2006).

The results of a school pupil survey conducted at 191 *Bremen schools* in 2003, confirms violence by teachers: not only the "everyday derision" but also physical violence und sexual assaults.[139]

Also impressive is the report on cases of violence by teachers, compiled by *Bachmann and Wolf* (2007), even though it does not meet scientific standards or claim to do so. On the occasion of experiences of their children with violence by teachers, these lady authors sought contacts with other affected families and founded a self-help initia-

---

[138] www.stern.de/panorama/schlaege-beleidigungen-mobbing-tabuthema ehrergewalt-616481.html 8. April 2008.

[139] www.stern.de/panorama/schlaege-beleidigungen-mobbing-tabuthema- lehrergewalt-616481.html of 8 April 2008 and www.emgs.de/literatur/default.html (request date: 8.3.2010).

tive in which they conducted numerous conversations with school pupils who were victims, and their parents. The summary of this report: even today, school pupils are put in a bad light, ostracized, subjected to psychological pressure and, in the worst case, physically abused by their teachers.

Clearly, there is a research gap and **need for research** with regard to the "taboo topic of violence by teachers" not only but also in the interest of the teachers and the schools. Only when this topic is directly and methodically addressed, will one have a chance to cast light on this dark field, compare "observations" with empirical findings and develop concepts for preventive measures.

3.4
Child and Youth Welfare as Place of Education and Prevention

"Offers and Facilities of Child and Youth Welfare (are) not insignificantly involved in the educational processes of children und adolescents of school age." (BMFSFJ 2005a, 233)

3.4.1
Child and Youth Welfare as place of education

As a further place of growing up and every-day upbringing, Child and Youth Welfare – with its areas of youth work, youth social work, children and youth protection, counselling in educational matters, support for young adults who have attained full age, appointment of an advisory guardian and custodianship as well as scope for interventions in the case of danger for children – addresses all persons under the age of 27, to lend them support in addition to that available from family and school and to contribute toward avoiding or eliminating disadvantages.[140]

The task and aspirations of Child and Youth Welfare are indisputable: they should and do wish to contribute to the facilitation of personality development and initiate and promote educational processes (Federal Ministry for Family, Seniors, Women and Youth (BMFSFJ)2005a, 233). Because: in Germany, all young people have a right to support of their development and upbringing to become independent and socially-adapted persons (§ 1 Social Security Code (SGB) VIII).

Youth Welfare is structured by the subsidiarity principle: at the local level, the officially recognised private entities of Youth Welfare with their offers take precedence over the Youth Welfare offices. The latter may not become active as public bodies with ultimate responsibility unless the private entities provide only insufficient offers or none at all to the young person in question. That the private entities of Youth Welfare in the municipalities get the first crack at solving any and all problems has supported the development and deployment of a heterogeneous offer of projects and

---

[140] The place of education "child day-care", which likewise lies in the area of responsibility of Child and Youth Welfare, is discussed in more detail in chapter 3.2.

programmes, for which the Child and Youth Welfare law just provides the framework (Holthusen/Schäfer 2007, 133).

Within the Child and Youth Welfare, it is particularly the offers of **Child and Youth work**[141] that play a key role in the everyday life of children and adolescents as predominantly non-formal learning locations outside school which enable the educational processes on the foundation of active involvement and participation.[142]

The publicly subsidised youth work focuses on children and adolescents in school-going age and among others encompasses the public youth work in youth leisure-time facilities, the offerings and activities of youth organisations as well as international youth initiative projects (BBE 2008, 78). Describing the tasks of the **youth work, §** 11, Par. 3 of the KJHG states the following: "general, political, social, health, cultural, natural and technical education", but also "sport, play and sociability" as well as "international youth work". More than 80% of the publicly subsidised measures in youth work are rendered by clubs, associations and initiatives, as private sponsors of the Youth Welfare.

Rauschenberg (2009a, 183f.) quite rightly points out that this other place of education, which has no direct affinity to school, does however have significant biographical relevance: "For many, youth work played a certain role in childhood and youth; perhaps it also represented an important station on the way toward becoming an adult ... the one or other politician, businessman and manager; the one or other professional sportsman, musician or artist and also the one or other scientist (might) have gained essential, perhaps even decisive impulses and suggestions for their subsequent careers, far away from school, in peer groups or in Youth Work."

Within this context, the "educational effects" of **voluntary commitment,** by means of active participation in clubs, associations and initiatives, deserve special mention[143]: in 2007, approximately 36% of the 16 to 21 year olds took on responsibilities in clubs and associations and an additional 32% took part in activities at least once a week. Even more widely spread is participation in "social interaction clubs": approx. 56% of the 16 to 21 year olds regularly participated in the offerings of sport clubs, hometown

---

[141] In the entire range of services of Child and Youth Welfare, the services of youth and youth social work are the services directly related to educational tasks, however they are directed to the respective specific target groups as well as needs and interests (Federal Ministry for Family, Seniors, Women and Youth (BMFSFJ)2005a, 234).

[142] **Volunteer services** is another sector of non-formal education where, among others, the volunteer social year and volunteer ecological year have been in demand more and more in recent years: in 1996/97 approx. 9,950 young adults completed such a year; in 2007/08 it was more than 18,000 (BBE 2008, 79).

[143] In this regard and concerning the importance of voluntary commitment in general, also see the expert report on the main topic of the 13th German Congress on Crime Prevention 2008 "Commited Citizens – Safe Society" (Steffen 2009b).
Nils Neuber will be speaking at the **15ᵗʰ German Congress on Crime Prevention** on the topic of "Educational Potentials in Sports".

clubs, citizens' groups and the like or took on different functions or administrative duties. Correspondingly lower, with a share of 22% of this age group – was the commitment in special interests and public welfare oriented clubs and associations (BBE 2008, 79). However, with the regard to utilisation of these learning locations outside school, differences owing to the **background of the persons** can be recognised: All in all, the greater a person's level of formal education, the greater the probability that this person actively participated in the educational opportunities of voluntary commitment (BBE 2008, 80).

Nevertheless: voluntary commitment is an important and sustainable societal learning field for young people. Here adolescents can have learning experiences which are not available anywhere else in this form. Adults who were active in an honorary capacity in their youth have more competences, are politically more committed and also consider themselves to be more successful professionally than those who were not active in an honorary capacity in their youth.[144]

However, there is a trend pointing to an unmistakable **decrease in significance** of youth work: the offer of publicly subsidised measures has declined and the number of measures per person, as well as the money spent on youth work, has gone down. It "remains to be seen to which extent the expansion of the extracurricular offerings at all-day schools will be at the expense of traditional child and youth work." (BBE 2008, 78; see above Chapter 3.3.1)[145]

Within the scope of Child and Youth Welfare an additional educational offer is provided by **youth social work,** with its school and career-related offerings. In the holistic and lifeworld-oriented child and Youth Welfare, youth social work plays a central role in conveying key qualifications as the prerequisite for successful, individual and societal integration. Its offerings should cover a broad basis: "The main target groups are disadvantaged adolescents who are limited in their societal participation possibilities owing to individual or social reasons. Youth social work helps school-weary adolescents, vocational training dropouts as well as adolescents without school and vocational training qualifications." (Federal Ministry for Family, Seniors, Women and Youth (BMFSFJ)2005a, 262). **School-related social work**[146], should contribute

---

[144] Thus the result of an empirical study on the learning potential of voluntary commitment, conducted between 2003 and 2007, in the DJI/TU Dortmund research association (DJI topic 2008/08).

[145] *Rauschenbach* (2009, 189) is somewhat more optimistic regarding the role youth work is able to play in the present day as well as in future, stating that this has not yet been clarified, and he rather tends to see the expansion of the extracurricular offerings at all-day schools positively: while it is true that youth work is at risk of "clearly losing social significance for children and adolescents, in the face of social change," it could definitely also have a future: within the context of the all-day schools, as a "contact point regarding school cooperational partnerships," linking this to their "education-related roots."

[146] **Dieter Doelling and Dieter Hermann** will be speaking at the **15th German Congress on the Prevention of Crime** on the topic of "Social Work at School – Crime Prevention Impact and Opportunities for Improvement".

toward enabling school success-stories for adolescents with individual problems or in socially disadvantaged life circumstances – in the course of their schooltime, it is presumed that every fourth child has some kind of problem with school (Federal Ministry for Family, Seniors, Women and Youth (BMFSFJ) 2005a, 262). Whether and how school-related social work functions, which specific educational services it is able to perform: to date there is no clear evaluation on this. However, this is hardly possible in the strict sense of research of impact, since education is also always self-education, a subjective performance that is built up in a biographically-cumulative manner and cannot be causally attributed to any individual place of learning (BMFSFJ 2005a, 269).[147]

3.4.2
Child and Youth Welfare as place of prevention of violence

From the areas of Child and Youth Welfare, **youth work** addresses all children and adolescents, without requiring that some kind of danger or threat be present or even just discernable. Hence, according to the understanding of what crime prevention means that is advocated here, youth work does not belong to the strategic approach with regard to the prevention of violence (see above chapter 2.2), but rather is to be viewed as universal prevention, and as such is one of the strategies and measures which can also have a crime prevention effect, but should not and ought not to have its primary focus on this, nor should it be reduced to this crime prevention aspect. This also applies precisely because of the development that has been noted for numerous years now in which normal, conventional youth work is now conducted under the label of "crime prevention" – because only then will it receive financial support![148]

However, apart from this, **prevention** is one of the **structural principles** of Child and Youth Welfare work:[149] Youth Welfare does not wait for impacts or harm to occur before it acts, but tries to ward off threats and hazards early on. In this context, the **prevention of violence** is just one task alongside others, but its greatest "flaw" and disadvantage[150] is its dependence on individual spectacular events and the ensuing public discussions: "In times of low "violence levels", the violence prevention approaches of the Child and Youth Welfare are under greater pressure to justify their work

---

[147] *Rauschenbach* (2009a, 208ff.) asks whether youth social work is not rather about reparation than about education; that its task does not lie in education but primarily in re-alignment to education and draws the conclusion that youth social work, with its tasks ranging from school social work to the work with pupils refusing to attend school and integrational support as well as the offerings for adolescents with migrational background, right up to measures concerning youth vocational assistance, is "relatively" clearly "interwoven" into the formal, non-formal and informal education.

[148] In this regard, see Steffen 2002, 8 and Holthusen/Schäfer 207, 140 "in the meantime, some offerings which are normally called youth education or sports are also 'sold' as measures for preventing violence."

[149] Here and in the following, see Holthusen/Schäfer 2007, 134ff.

[150] Another problem is the great number of sponsors of Child and Youth Welfare in the municipalities and the corresponding heterogeneity, time limitations, discontinuity and dependence on extraneous considerations of the programmes and projects (Holthusen/Schäfer 2007, 133f.).

than, for example, are schools, the police and the judiciary. However, subsequent to dramatic events with powerful media echo, the "prevention of violence" label once again makes it easier to obtain financial support." (Holthusen/Schäfer 2007, 134)

With prevention, the **specific approach** of the Youth Welfare is on the one hand to be found in the principles of non-compulsion and participation, which are firmly anchored in Child and Youth Welfare – and with the cooperation with other partners, which not infrequently leads to irritations; on the other hand, the approach is to progress on the basis of the young person's resources and not to focus on his or her deficits. Not to focus one's attention just on violent behaviour but on the young person as a whole, and to accept this individual as a person, which, . however, does not mean that this person's violent behaviour is accepted (Holthusen/Schäfer 2007, 135f.; Heitkötter and others 2007, 263).

On the basis of this approach, the Child and Youth Welfare strategies can be classified as non-specific strategies with a violence prevention element and as selective, or indicated, strategies, or also "strategies for target groups with a direct proximity to violence" (according to the description by Holthusen/Schäfer 2007).

Non-specific strategies with a violence prevention element[151] are individual, group and community work that tend to focus on young age groups as well as legal guardians, that are oriented to the social area, that are in line with the resources of children and adolescents and organised in projects, which implies that they are limited both in content and duration. Apart from the curricular programmes that are, for the most part, standardised,[152] numerous projects build on the active participation and cooperation of the children and adolescents. Cooperation is primarily with the child day-care centres and the schools. For the most part, the lack of gender-specific alignment of the offerings is disappointing, as well as the finding that the cultural and social differences of the children are not consistently taken into account (Holthusen/Schäfer 2007, 143).

Selective or indicated strategies for target groups with a **direct proximity to violence** are on the one hand targeted at adolescents with a potential for violence, and on the other hand at adolescents who have already drawn attention to themselves with their violent behaviour. In both cases, though, violence is only seen as "a moment in the behaviour of children and adolescents. It can be an indicator for an educational need and this then is decisive for the selection of suitable offers" (Holthusen/Schäfer 2007, 143).[153]

---

[151] This also includes **youth media protection**, which aims to protect children and adolescents from media that endanger youth, that is, in this case, media depicting and glorifying violence. Educational youth protection is becoming more significant here: (media-) pedagogical offerings should enable children and adolescents to deal with the new media and their offers, and, should this be required, to obtain help (Holthusen/Schäfer 2007, 142).

[152] For instance "Faustlos" (without fists) (www.faustlos.de), where adolescents only have limited participation regarding participation in its design.

[153] With problematic family constellations the Youth Welfare can select **Help with Upbringing** from the

The **strategies focussed on endangerment** are aimed at young persons in situations in which adults suspect high risks of violence – here, not infrequently does Youth Welfare come into conflict with the different interests of adolescents and adults. One of Youth Welfare's core tasks is to support adolescents in such conflicts and to deescalate conflicts, in particular with the objective of viewing the adolescents' behaviour as typical for their age and not to label it as "violence" too soon. So, for instance, mobile youth work is focused "on adolescents, who are regarded from the perspective of public order are being disturbing, dissocial and thus in need of care … a normalising and non stigmatising look at young people and their formations of groups should become possible." (Holthusen/Schäfer 2007, 145f)[154]

The targeted groups of these projects tend to be adolescents rather than children and boys rather than girls, whereby there are hardly any boy-specific approaches. But in the meantime, there are more and more offers for adolescents with migrational background in which specialists or volunteer workers with a migrational background get involved, using their (inter-)cultural competences. Preference is given to work done in groups; the focus is not primarily on violence but particularly on the lifeworlds of minors, led by the thought of **participation**, which specifically simplifies access to "hard-to-reach" adolescents and youth groups (Holthusen/Schäfer 2007, 148).

Also with the strategies focussed on adolescents who have already drawn attention to themselves with their **violent behaviour** – or have become criminal – "Youth Welfare assumes that the pedagogical approaches can contribute toward reducing violent behaviour." (Holthusen/Schäfer 2007, 149)[155] In principle, providing help is preferred to punishment, educational support has preference over penal sanctions, informal procedures are preferable to formal procedures and ambulant measures should be used rather than stationary measures. Regardless, with strategies that are strongly aligned to the individual case, one can rather establish a deficit than resource-oriented approach and also the principles of non-compulsion and participation are (partially) given up – already owing to the requisite cooperation with the sanction system (Holthusen/Schäfer 2007, 151ff.).

All in all, though, in recent years, the development of Child and Youth Welfare, particularly also in the area of prevention of violence, has been characterised by efforts aimed at implementing the general principles of "non-compulsion" and "participation" – and "in future their success will also greatly depend on the extent to which they are able to make non-compulsion of participation and involvement of children and

---

entire spectrum and introduce the required measures (see Chapter 3.1 "Family")

[154] Examples for such strategies are e.g. the approach "We look after ourselves" (www.wir-kuemmern-uns-selbst.de) or also the fan projects (www.kos-fanprojekte.de).

[155] Examples for this are the **social training courses** where "integration" and "confrontation" are seen as key principles or also **Anti-Aggression training**, which also emphasizes "acceptance" and "confrontation" (Holthusen/Schäfer 2007, 151f.).

adolescents a continuously effective requirement which is accepted and recognised from all sides." (Heitkötter and others 2007,263).

Bibliography

Aktionsrat Bildung (Hrsg.)(2008): Bildungsrisiken und –chancen im Globalisierungsprozess. Jahresgutachten 2008. Wiesbaden.

Aktionsrat Bildung (Hrsg.)(2007): Bildungsgerechtigkeit. Jahresgutachten 2007. Wiesbaden.

Arbeitsstelle Kinder- und Jugendkriminalitätsprävention (Hrsg.) (2007): Strategien der Gewaltprävention im Kindes- und Jugendalter. München.

Arbeitsstelle Kinder- und Jugendkriminalitätsprävention (Hrsg.) (1999): Der Mythos der Monsterkids. Strafunmündige „Mehrfach- und Intensivtäter". Dokumentation des Hearings des Bundesjugendkuratoriums am 18. Juni 1998 in Bonn. München.

Autorengruppe Bildungsberichterstattung (Hrsg.)(2008): Bildung in Deutschland 2008. Ein indikatorengestützter Bericht mit einer Analyse zu Übergängen im Anschluss an den Sekundarbereich I. Bielefeld 2008.

Autorengruppe Bildungsberichterstattung (Hrsg.)(2006): Bildung in Deutschland 2006. Ein indikatorengestützter Bericht mit einer Analyse zur Migration. Bielefeld 2006.

Bachmann, Angelika/Wolf, Patricia (2007): Wenn Lehrer schlagen. Die verschwiegene Gewalt an unseren Schulen. München.

Baier, Dirk u.a. (2009): Jugendliche in Deutschland als Opfer und Täter von Gewalt. Erster Forschungsbericht zum gemeinsamen Forschungsprojekt des Bundesministeriums des Innern und des KFN. Forschungsbericht Nr. 107. Hannover.

Baier, Dirk u.a. (2006): Schülerbefragung 2005: Gewalterfahrungen, Schulschwänzen und Medienkonsum von Kindern und Jugendlichen. KFN-Materialien für die Praxis – Nr. 2.Hannover.

Bannenberg, Britta (2010): Amok. Ursachen erkennen – Warnsignale verstehen – Katastrophen verhindern. Gütersloh.

BBE siehe Autorengruppe Bildungsberichterstattung

Beelmann, Andreas (2009): Prävention von Kinder- und Jugendkriminalität: Aktuelle Probleme und Ergebnisse der internationalen Erfolgsforschung. In: BMJ (Hrsg.) 2009, S. 257-274.

Bergmann, Wolfgang/Hüther, Gerald (2007): Computersüchtig. Kinder im Sog der neuen Medien. Düsseldorf.

Bertelsmann-Stiftung (Hrsg.)(2008): Integration braucht faire Bildungschancen. Gütersloh.

Bertelsmann-Stiftung (Hrsg.)(2006): Interkulturelle Kompetenz – Schlüsselkompetenz des 21. Jahrhunderts? Gütersloh.

Bertram, Hans (2009): Familienwandel in der Erziehung. In: Schwind/Steffen/Hermann (Hrsg.) 2009, S. 30-33.

Betz, Tanja/ Rother, Pia (2008): Frühe Kindheit im Fokus der Politik. In: DJI Bulletin 81, S. 11-12.

BJK siehe Bundesjugendkuratorium BMBF siehe Bundesministerium für Bildung und Forschung

BMFSFJ siehe Bundesministerium für Familie, Senioren, Frauen und Jugend

BMJ siehe Bundesministerium der Justiz

Bock-Famulla, Kathrin (2008): Länderreport Frühkindliche Bildungssysteme 2008. Hrsg. von der Bertelsmann-Stiftung. Gütersloh.

Bos, Wilfried/Wendt, Heike (2008): Bildungsungerechtigkeit in Deutschland. Zur Situation von Kindern und Jugendlichen mit Migrationshintergrund. In: Bertelsmann-Stiftung (Hrsg.) 2008, S. 47-65.

Bundesarbeitsgemeinschaft der Kinderschutz-Zentren e.V. (Hrsg.) (2009): Frühe Hilfen. Köln.

Bundesjugendkuratorium (Hrsg.)(2009): Kinderarmut in Deutschland. Eine drängende Herausforderung an die Politik. München.

Bundesjugendkuratorium (Hrsg.)(2008): Zukunftsfähigkeit von Kindertagesstätten. München.

Bundesjugendkuratorium (Hrsg.)(2004a): Bildung fängt vor der Schule an. Bonn.

Bundesjugendkuratorium (Hrsg.)(2004b): Neue Bildungsorte für Kinder und Jugendliche. Bonn.

Bundesjugendkuratorium (Hrsg.)(2003): Auf dem Weg zu einer neuen Schule. Jugendhilfe und Schule in gemeinsamer Verantwortung. Bonn/Berlin.

Bundesjugendkuratorium (Hrsg.)(2002): Bildung ist mehr als Schule – Leipziger Thesen zur aktuellen bildungspolitischen Debatte. Bonn/ Berlin/Leipzig, 10. Juli 2002.

Bundesministerium für Bildung und Forschung (Hrsg.)(2009a): Aufstieg durch Bildung. Die Qualifizierungsinitiative für Deutschland. Berlin.

Bundesministerium für Bildung und Forschung (Hrsg.)(2009b): Lernen vor Ort. Eine gemeinsame Initiative des Bundesministeriums für Bildung und Forschung mit deutschen Stiftungen. Bonn, Berlin.

Bundesministerium für Familie, Senioren, Frauen und Jugend (Hrsg.) (2009a): 13. Kinder- und Jugendbericht. Bericht über die Lebenssituation junger Menschen und die Leistungen der Kinder- und Jugendhilfe in Deutschland. Berlin.

Bundesministerium für Familie, Senioren, Frauen und Jugend (Hrsg.) (2009b): FamilienReport 2009. Berlin.

Bundesministerium für Familie, Senioren, Frauen und Jugend (Hrsg.) (2005a): Zwölfter Kinder- und Jugendbericht. Bericht über die Lebenssituation junger Menschen und die Leistungen der Kinder- und Jugendhilfe in Deutschland. Berlin.

Bundesministerium für Familie, Senioren, Frauen und Jugend (Hrsg.) (2005b): Stärkung familialer Beziehungs- und Erziehungskompetenzen. Berlin.

Bundesministerium für Familie, Senioren, Frauen und Jugend (Hrsg.) (2005c): Nationaler Aktionsplan. Für ein kindergerechtes Deutschland 2005 – 2010. Berlin.

Bundesministerium der Justiz (Hrsg.)(2009): Das Jugendkriminalrecht vor neuen Herausforderungen? Jenaer Symposium 9.-11. September 2008. Mönchengladbach.

Bundesverband der Unfallkassen (Hrsg.)(2005): Gewalt an Schulen. Ein empiri-

scher Beitrag zum gewaltverursachten Verletzungsgeschehen an Schulen in
Deutschland 1993-2003. München.

Buskotte, Andrea (2007): Am Rande der Wahrnehmung. Kinder als Zeugen und
Opfer häuslicher Gewalt (www.praeventionstag.de).

Bussmann, Kai (2005): Verbot elterlicher Gewalt gegen Kinder – Auswirkungen des
Rechts auf gewaltfreie Erziehung. In: Deegener, G./ Körner, W. (Hrsg.): Kindes-
misshandlung und Vernachlässigung. Ein Handbuch. Göttingen e.a., S. 243-258.

Deutsche Telekom Stiftung (2010): Frühe Bildung auf dem Prüfstand. Welchen
Stellenwert nimmt frühkindliche Bildung in den Köpfen der Gesellschaft
wirklich ein? Bonn.

Deutsches Jugendinstitut (2010): DJI-Thema 2008/09 „Fürs Leben lernen: Nachhal-
tige Kompetenzen durch informelle Bildung".

Deutsches Jugendinstitut (2009a): Quantität braucht Qualität. Agenda für den qualitativ
orientierten Ausbau der Kindertagesbetreuung für unter Dreijährige. München.

Deutsches Jugendinstitut (2009b): DJI-Thema 2009/2 „Kinderbetreuung zwischen
Familie, Kindertagespflege und Kita: neue Zahlen und Entwicklungen".

Deutsches Jugendinstitut (2009c): DJI Bulletin 85 „Das Wissen über Kinder – eine
Bilanz empirischer Studien". 1/2009.

Deutsches Jugendinstitut (2009d): Stellungnahme des Deutschen Jugendinstitutes
zur öffentlichen Anhörung der Kinderkommission zum Thema „Neue Kon-
zepte Früher Hilfen" am 2. März 2009.

Deutsches Jugendinstitut (2009e): DJI Bulletin 88 „Experiment Familie". 4/2009.

Deutsches Jugendinstitut (2008a): DJI Bulletin 81 „Gerechtes Aufwachsen ermögli-
chen. Bildung –Integration – Teilhabe". 1/2008.

Deutsches Jugendinstitut (2008b): DJI-Thema 2008/12 „Gut integriert? Fakten und
Emotionen".

Deutsches Jugendinstitut (2007): DJI Bulletin 80 „Kindertagesbetreuung in Deutschland. 3/4/2007.

DJI siehe Deutsches Jugendinstitut

Erthal, Claudia/Bussmann, Kai (2009): Alltägliche Gewalt in der Erziehung. In:
Schwind/Steffen/Hermann (Hrsg.) 2009, S. 37-56.

Feltes, Thomas/Goldberg, Brigitta (2009): Gewalt und Gewaltprävention in der
Schule. Holzkirchen/Obb.

Galm, Beate u.a. (2007): Kindeswohl und Kindeswohlgefährdung. In: Arbeitsstelle
Kinder- und Jugendkriminalitätsprävention (Hrsg.): Strategien der Gewaltprävention im Kindes- und Jugendalter. München. S. 31-59.

Geißler, Rainer/Weber-Menges, Sonja (2008): Migrantenkinder im Bildungssystem:
doppelt benachteiligt. APuZ 49/2008, S. 14-22.

Gragert, Nicola u.a. (2008): Angebote der Kinder- und Jugendhilfe als Beitrag zur
Teilhabe. In: DJI Bulletin 81, 1/2008, S. 30-31.

Groebel, Jo (2009):Medien als (Mit-)Erzieher im Digitalzeitalter. In: Schwind/Stef-
fen/Hermann (Hrsg.) 2009, S. 58-85.

Hanke, Ottmar (2007): Strategien der Gewaltprävention an Schulen. In: Arbeitsstelle Kinder- und Jugendkriminalitätsprävention (Hrsg.): Strategien der Gewaltprävention im Kindes- und Jugendalter. München. S. 104-130.

Heitkötter, Martina (2009): Öffentliche Betreuung und Familie – Spannungsfeld oder Ergänzung? In: DJI Bulletin 85. 1/2009, S. 18-21.

Heitkötter, Martina u.a. (2007): Unterstützende Rahmenbedingungen gewaltpräventiver Strategien. In: Arbeitsstelle Kinder- und Jugendkriminalitätsprävention (Hrsg.): Strategien der Gewaltprävention im Kindes- und Jugendalter. München. S. 248-278.

Heitmeyer, Wilhelm (Hrsg.)(2010): Deutsche Zustände. Folge 8. Frankfurt am Main.

Heynen, Susanne (2007): Strategien zur Prävention von Kindeswohlgefährdung bei Partnergewalt. In: Arbeitsstelle Kinder- und Jugendkriminalitätsprävention (Hrsg.): Strategien der Gewaltprävention im Kindes- und Jugendalter. München. S. 60-73.

Holthusen, Bernd/Schäfer, Heiner (2007): Strategien der Gewaltprävention in der Kinder- und Jugendhilfe im Jugendalter. In: Arbeitsstelle Kinder- und Jugendkriminalitätsprävention (Hrsg.): Strategien der Gewaltprävention im Kindes- und Jugendalter. München. S. 131-168.

Hübenthal, Maksim (2009): Kinderarmut in Deutschland. Empirische Befunde, kinderpolitische Akteure und gesellschaftspolitische Handlungsstrategien. Expertise im Auftrag des Deutschen Jugendinstitutes. München.

Hüther, Gerald (2009): Männer. Das schwache Geschlecht und sein Gehirn. Göttingen.

Hüther, Gerald u.a. (1999): Die neurobiologische Verankerung psychosozialer Erfahrungen. Zeitschrift für Psychosomatische Medizin und Psychotherapie. H. 45, S. 2-17.

Jurczyk, Karin/Heitkötter, Martina (2007): Kindertagespflege in Bewegung. In: DJI Bulletin 80, 3/4/2007, S. 20-22.

Keupp, Heiner (2009): Urvertrauen zum Leben. Wie man die Gesundheit von Kindern und Jugendlichen fördern kann. Blätter der Wohlfahrtspflege 6/2009, S. 214-220.

Kindler, Heinz (2007): Beeinträchtigung des Kindeswohls durch häusliche Gewalt (www.praeventionstag.de).

Klemm, Klaus (2009): Klassenwiederholungen – teuer und unwirksam. Studie im Auftrag der Bertelsmann Stiftung. Gütersloh.

Klemm, Klaus/Klemm, Annemarie (2010): Ausgaben für Nachhilfe – teurer und unfairer Ausgleich für fehlende individuelle Förderung. Studie im Auftrag der Bertelsmann Stiftung. Gütersloh.

Koalitionsvertrag zwischen CDU, CSU und FDP (2009): Wachstum. Bildung. Zusammenhalt. (17. Legislaturperiode). Berlin.

Kraus, Josef (2008): Bildungsgerechtigkeit. APuZ 49/2008, S. 8-13.

Krumm, Volker/Weiß, Susanne (2006): Ungerechte Lehrer. Zu einem Defizit in der Forschung über Gewalt an Schulen. In: Melzer, W. (Hrsg.) 2006, S. 123-146.

Krumm, Volker u.a. (1997): Gewalt in der Schule – auch von Lehrern. Empirische

Pädagogik (1997) 2, S. 257-275 und: www.paedpsych.jk.uni-linz.ac.at:4711/
LEHRTEXTE/Krumm.html.

Lange, Andreas/Jurczyk, Karin (2009): Die globalisierte Familie. DJI Bulletin 88.
4/2009, S. 4-6.

Lengning, Anke/Zimmermann, Peter (2009): Expertise Intervention und Präventi-
onsmaßnahmen im Bereich früher Hilfen. Internationaler Forschungsstand,
Evaluationsstandards und Empfehlungen für die Umsetzung in Deutschland.
Hrsg. Nationales Zentrum Frühe Hilfen. Köln.

Lösel, Friedrich (2006): Bestandsaufnahme und Evaluation von Angeboten im
Elternbildungsbereich (publikationen@bundesregierung.de).

Lösel, Friedrich (2004): Multimodale Gewaltprävention bei Kindern und Jugendlichen:
Familie, Kindergarten, Schule. In: Melzer/Schwind (Hrsg.) 2004, S. 326-348.

Lösel, Friedrich u.a. (2010): Das Präventionsprogramm EFFEKT (1. Teil). In: forum
kriminalprävention 1/2010, S. 39-48.

Lösel, Friedrich u.a. (2008): Das Präventionsprogramm EFFEKT: Entwicklungsför-
derung in Familien: Eltern- und Kinder-Training. In: Bundesministerium des
Innern (Hrsg.): Theorie und Praxis gesellschaftlichen Zusammenhalts. Berlin
2008, S. 199-219.

Lucas, Torsten (2009): „Wenn der Blitz einschlägt…" Trauma, Entwicklung und
Resilienz. In: Bundesarbeitsgemeinschaft 2009, S. 114- 128.

Lenzen, Dieter (2009): Eine neue Chance für die Bildung? APuZ 45/2009, S. 6-9.

Meier-Gräwe, Uta (2009): Der tiefgreifende Strukturwandel von Familie und Kindheit –
Neue Herausforderungen für Kindertageseinrichtungen. In: DJI-Thema 2009/2.

Melzer, Wolfgang (Hrsg.)(2006): Gewalt an Schulen. Analyse und Prävention. Gießen.

Melzer, Wolfgang (2004): Von der Analyse zur Prävention – Gewaltprävention in
der Praxis. In: Melzer/Schwind (Hrsg.) 2004, S. 35-49.

Melzer, Wolfgang/Schubarth, Wilfried/Ehninger, Frank (2004): Gewaltprävention und
Schulentwicklung. Analysen und Handlungskonzepte. Bad Heilbrunn/Obb.

Melzer, Wolfgang/Schwind, Hans-Dieter (Hrsg.)(2004): Gewaltprävention in der
Schule. Grundlagen – Praxismodelle –Perspektiven. Dokumentation des 15.
Mainzer Opferforums 2003. Baden-Baden.

Menne, Klaus (2009): Familie und Erziehungsberatung – ein nicht artikulierter Skan-
dal. Theorie und Praxis der Sozialen Arbeit. Nr. 5/2009 (60. Jg.), S. 365-373.

Meyer-Timpe, Ulrike (2008): Unsere armen Kinder. Wie Deutschland seine Zukunft
verspielt. München.

Mückenberger, Ulrich (2009): Die Familie darf nicht länger Privatproblem der
Eltern sein. DJI Bulletin 88. 2009e, S. 10-11.

NRW-Landesverbände AWO, DGB, GEW, Deutscher Kinderschutzbund, Pari-
tätischer Wohlfahrtsverband (2010): Memorandum zur Bekämpfung der
Kinderarmut – eine Bündnisstrategie. Theorie und Praxis der Sozialen Arbeit
Nr. 1/2010 (61.Jg.), S. 65-69.

Peuckert, Rüdiger (2007): Zur aktuellen Lage der Familie. In: Ecarius, Jutta (Hrsg.):

Handbuch Familie. Wiesbaden 2007, S. 36-56.

Programm Innere Sicherheit. Fortschreibung 2008/2009. Hrsg. Von der Ständigen Konferenz der Innenminister und –senatoren der Länder (www.bundestag.de).

Rauschenbach, Thomas (2009a): Zukunftschance Bildung. Familie, Jugendhilfe und Schule in neuer Allianz. Weilheim und München.

Rauschenbach, Thomas (2009b): Neue Realitäten, alte Ideale. DJI Bulletin 88. 2009e, S. 3.

Rauschenbach, Thomas (2009c): Bildung – eine ambivalente Herausforderung für die Soziale Arbeit? SP Soziale Passagen. 2009/1, S. 209-255.

Rauschenbach, Thomas (2007): Kindertagesbetreuung in Deutschland – eine empirische Standortbestimmung. DJI Bulletin 80. 3/4/2007, S. 5-10.

Roth, Gerhard (2008): Homo neuro-biologicus – ein neues Menschenbild? APuZ 44-45/2008, S. 6-12.

Sann, Alexandra/Schäfer, Reinhild (2008): Frühe Hilfen zwischen Helfen und Kontrollieren. DJI Bulletin 81. 1/2008, S. 25-27.

Sann, Alexandra/Thrum, Kathrin (2008): Stärkung der Erziehung in der Familie – Chancen und Grenzen der Arbeit mit Laien. DJI Bulletin 81. 1/2008, S. 18-19.

Scheithauer, Herbert/Mayer, Heidrun (2009): Außerfamiliale Erziehung in Krippe und Kindergarten: Papilio - ein Programm im Kindergarten zur Primärprävention von Verhaltensproblemen und zur Förderung sozial-emotionaler Kompetenz. In: Schwind/Steffen/Hermann (Hrsg.) 2009, S. 69-85.

Scheithauer, Herbert/Mayer, Heidrun (2008): Papilio: Ein Programm zur entwicklungsorientierten Primärprävention von Verhaltensproblemen und Förderung sozial-emotionaler Kompetenzen im Kindergarten. In: Bundesministerium des Innern (Hrsg.): Theorie und Praxis gesellschaftlichen Zusammenhalts. Berlin 2008, S. 221-239.

Schneider, Ilona K. (2009): Lernfenster Kindergarten. APuZ 45/2009, S. 32-38.

Schubarth, Wilfried (2010): Gewalt und Mobbing an Schulen. Möglichkeiten der Prävention und Intervention. Stuttgart.

Schubarth, Wilfried (2006): Gewaltprävention durch Öffnung von Schule. Schule und Jugendhilfe – gemeinsam zum Wohle des Kindes. In: Melzer, W. (Hrsg.) 2006, S. 181-192.

Schubarth, Wilfried (2004): Schulsozialarbeit und Unterstützungsnetzwerke für Schulen –Perspektiven einer „systemischen Gewaltprävention/-intervention". In: Melzer/Schwind (Hrsg.) 2004, S. 243-253.

Schwind, Hans-Dieter (2009): Familiale Erziehung aus kriminologischer Sicht. In: Schwind/Steffen/Hermann (Hrsg.) 2009, S. 19-29.

Schwind, Hans-Dieter/Baumann, Jürgen (Hrsg.)(1990): Ursachen, Prävention und Kontrolle von Gewalt. Analysen und Vorschläge der unabhängigen Regierungskommission zur Verhinderung und Bekämpfung von Gewalt. 4 Bde. Berlin.

Schwind, H-D./Steffen, W./Hermann, D. (Hrsg.)(2009): Kriminalprävention durch familiale Erziehung? Dokumentation des 19. Mainzer Opferforums 2008.

Baden-Baden.

Sommerfeld, Verena (2007): Strategien der Gewaltprävention im Bereich der Kindertageseinrichtungen. In: Arbeitsstelle Kinder- und Jugendkriminalitätsprävention (Hrsg.): Strategien der Gewaltprävention im Kindes- und Jugendalter. München. 2007. S. 74-103.

Stecher, Ludwig u.a. (Hrsg.)(2009): Ganztägige Bildung und Betreuung. Zeitschrift für Pädagogik. 54. Beiheft 2009.

Steffen, Wiebke (2009a): Ergebnisse des 19.Opferforums des Weißen Ringes 2008 „Kriminalprävention durch familiale Erziehung?" – Zusammenfassung der Referate und Diskussionen. In: Schwind/Steffen/ Hermann (Hrsg.) 2009, S. 161-166.

Steffen, Wiebke (2009b): Bürgerschaftliches Engagement in der Kriminalprävention. Gutachten zum 13. Deutschen Präventionstag „Engagierte Bürger – sichere Gesellschaft". In: E. Marks/W. Steffen (Hrsg.): Engagierte Bürger – sichere Gesellschaft. Ausgewählte Beiträge des 13. Deutschen Präventionstages 2008. Mönchengladbach 2009, S. 25-72.

Steffen, Wiebke (2009c): Moderne Gesellschaften und Kriminalität. Der Beitrag der Kriminalprävention zu Integration und Solidarität. Gutachten für den 14. Deutschen Präventionstag am 8. und 9. Juni 2009 in Hannover (www.bundestag.de).

Steffen, Wiebke (2008): Jugendkriminalität und ihre Verhinderung zwischen Wahrnehmung und empirischen Befunden. Gutachten zum 12. Deutschen Präventionstag am 18. und 19. Juni 2007 in Wiesbaden. In: E. Marks/W. Steffen (Hrsg.): Starke Jugend – starke Zukunft. Ausgewählte Beiträge des 12. Deutschen Präventionstages 2007. Mönchengladbach 2008, S. 233-272.

Steffen, Wiebke (2002): Zukünftige Aufgaben der Polizei: Kriminalprävention als Gefahr und Chance. In: Polizei Dein Partner. Gewerkschaft der Polizei – Junge Gruppe. 11. Bundesjugendkonferenz 2002, S. 7-9.

Stöbe-Blossey, Sybille (Hrsg.)(2010): Kindertagesbetreuung im Wandel. Perspektiven für die Organisationsentwicklung. Wiesbaden.

Textor, Martin R. (2009): Elternarbeit im Kindergarten. Ziele, Formen, Methoden. Norderstedt.

Thiessen, Barbara (2009): Fremde Familien. DJI Bulletin 88. 4/2009, S. 7-9.

Uslucan, Haci-Halil (2009): Riskante Bedingungen des Aufwachsens: Erhöhte Gewaltanfälligkeit junger Migranten? In: BMJ 2009, S. 187-202.

von der Leyen, Ursula (2009): Grundsatzreferat zur Familienpolitik. In: Schwind/ Steffen/Hermann (Hrsg.) 2009, S. 150-159.

Wetzels, Peter (2009): Erziehungsstile und Wertorientierungen in Familien mit und ohne Migrationshintergrund. In: Schwind/Steffen/Hermann (Hrsg.) 2009, S. 102-119.

Wößmann, Ludger (2008): Die Bildungsfinanzierung in Deutschland im Licht der Lebenszyklusperspektive: Gerechtigkeit im Widerstreit mit Effizienz? Zeitschrift für Erziehungswissenschaften 11. Jg. (2008) H. 2, S. 214-233.

German Congress on Crime Prevention and Conference Partners

Berlin Declaration of the 15th German Congress on Crime Prevention

Education and qualification are the prerequisites for social participation and individual opportunities in life. In Germany, however, educational success is quite significantly determined by social class and background. Income, educational and integrational poverty, as well as the experience of social injustice and social exclusion, can favour crime, especially violent crime. For this reason educational equality and equal opportunities for access to education also contribute to the prevention of violence and crime.

The education of the coming generation is one of the key future tasks of our society. That is why the 15th German Congress on Crime Prevention "Education –Prevention –Future" has made this its central topic of focus and thus taken up and elaborated on a complex of problems which had already become apparent at the discussions of the 14th German Congress on Crime Prevention: the interaction of educational equality, integration and social participation regarding the emergence and, to an even larger extent, prevention of violent crime.

On the foundation of the expert appraisal of Dr. Wiebke Steffen "Lern- und Lebensräume von children und Jugendlichen als Orte von Bildung and Gewaltprävention" (Learning and Living Spaces of Children and Young Adults as Places for Education and Prevention of Violence) on the topic in focus, the German Congress on Crime Prevention, its permanent conference partners as well as its partner, which is hosting this year's event, hereby issue the "Berlin Declaration".

Changes in society and their social consequences adversely affect educational equality in Germany: educational success is determined by social class and background to a great extent, and therefore social inequality is inherited

- Modernisation processes have led to a situation in which children and juveniles are presently growing up in a society which is characterised on the one hand by the pluralisation of lifestyles, value systems and objectives and on the other hand by life opportunities and situations that are formed by social structures in vastly different ways.

- These changes involve opportunities but also risks. Most children and young adults are able to master the challenges without any major conspicuousness and are well able to find their place in life. On the other hand, however, there also are young persons who are not able to utilise life's opportunities; those who are unable to cope and fail as a result of the risks.

- This is because the conditions for self-determined utilisation of the chances presuppose resources that are not accessible for these children and young adults. This applies in particular to children and juveniles of the lower social classes –

including many with a migration background. These risk groups include at least one fifth and up to one quarter of all young persons.

- Currently the educational systems are still not sufficiently able to break down these disadvantages. Risk situations lead to a clear deterioration of educational opportunities. In Germany the problem of inequality due to a different background still remains – and therefore also the related discussion regarding equal opportunities and educational equality.

Education is more than school: learning and living spaces of children and young adults as places of education

- Education is more than school. It is a continual process in the course of life which takes place at numerous stations in the lives of children und young adults. However, it is evidently less and less certain that the educational effects of these learning and living spaces can be secured for all young persons. For this reason young people also cannot fall back on the educationally relevant resources that are necessary for success at school.

- Much that is attributed to schools, both positive and negative, both successes as well as failures is by no means solely or even predominantly to be attributed to schools alone. Formal education, namely schools, can only function when the places of education function in the forefront and alongside the schools. This applies particularly to the educational places of family, day care facilities for children, as well as the offers and facilities for children and youth welfare. These places of education are – in conjunction with schools –relevant for the upbringing and education of virtually all children, and of equal importance. Hence, they should also be related to one another and cooperate with one another.

- Family plays a decisive role in the success of learning and educational processes; and this success significantly depends on the family's social background and life circumstances. The influence of the family is so great that it is very hard for inequalities to be compensated for by means of support systems and educational institutions later on. For this reason the family must be recognised and strengthened as a place of education if the subsequent measures aimed at advancing education are not to be in vain.

- Child care at day care centres, growing up in public responsibility, is a path that can be taken to compensate for disadvantages through early access to educational places and educationally supportive life environments that are organised publicly and for which the public is responsible. What is more, the other offers and facilities for children and juvenile support also play a significant role in the educational trajectories of children and young adults of school-going age, and play a key role as extra-curricular places of learning which facilitate educational processes on the foundation of active participation and co-operation.

Education is prevention, prevention is education

- As spaces for learning and living, places of education for children and young adults are at the same time also places where acts of violence can occur and where violence can be prevented. Strategies, programmes and measures for the prevention of violence in childhood and juvenile age can therefore also be understood and described under the aspect of education.

- On the one hand, all forms of violence prevention that are focussed on persons are educational objectives, because they are targeted at the development of the personality, the formation of identity or the acquisition of abilities to act. On the other hand, most of the strategies developed in recent years can be described as pedagogical strategies. This orientation does justice to the fact that it is a question of preventing violence in the course of childhood and adolescence, and that instances of such violence or of the mere threat of such violence can be understood as opportunities for learning and, as the case may be, also as opportunities for providing pedagogical support.

- Violence preventive strategies within the family are predominantly aimed at the parents and have the objective of strengthening and promoting their parenting and relationship competences, and thus (also) of preventing children from becoming victims of parental violence, which lead to considerable problems regarding the children's future development. However, in the child day care facilities, at school and also in the offers and facilities for children and young adults, it is particularly the young persons on whom the measures, programmes and strategies are focussed.

- The positive development observed in recent years regarding the occurrence of violent crime in the life of children and young adults in general, but also at the four places of education that have been analysed here, namely family, children day care facilities, school and facilities for children and juveniles confirms the pedagogical alignment of violence prevention, just as its importance for integration and social participation of the children and young adults.

The German Congress on Crime Prevention appeals to the responsible persons in politics and in the media, as well as in civil society groupings at communal, state and federal levels:

1. To take note of and respect the contribution of the increasingly pedagogically aligned violence and crime prevention offers for integration and social participation and to support and extend this proven path for pointing out and clarifying socially binding standards and values.

2. To continue to make every effort to support the families in their educational and relationship competences; to decisively combat the causes of poverty and discrimination and to facilitate providing children and their families with an adequate

standard of living as well as opportunities to participate in society. Given the significance of the measures for early encouragement and early assistance, it is necessary to avoid perfected control systems, to respect the parents' right to bring up their children and to rely on voluntariness and participation.

3. Further expand the day-care offers for children, whereat one does, however, have to be sure not to place great expectations on these facilities for early, individually-oriented advancement which they are presently not able to meet at all, given the currently applicable framework conditions. Parents have to become more intensively and systematically involved in the upbringing and educational processes of the child day care facilities. The objective is to expand these facilities so that they become centres for integrated service offers that are readily accessible to their realistically defined target groups.

4. To force the erection and expansion of schools to all-day schools, in particular also with the objective of supplementing the conventional teaching schools with other curricula and forms of learning. The educational systems are to be further developed with regard to a strengthening of the principles of individual advancement and support, the expansion of available all-day offers and the networking of formal and informal education. In order to achieve this, not only should one strive to attain the cooperation of children and young adults, but also to succeed at creating new places of education, right up to local alliances for education and communal educational infrastructures.

5. To undertake all efforts needed in order to establish educational equality as the prerequisite for individual opportunities in life and participation in society, and thus also for the prevention of violence and crime.

In this regard, the 15th German Congress on Crime Prevention refers to the discussions of the 12th, 13th and 14th German Congress on Crime Prevention, the demands and appeals of the "Wiesbaden Declaration", the "Leipzig Declaration" and the "Hanover Declaration." Their topicality and urgency continue unabated.

Berlin, 11th of May 2010

Lectures and Documents from the 5th Annual International Forum

Jürgen Stock

International Cybercrime: Results from the Annual International Forum[1]

The objective of this contribution is to give account of the findings and results achieved during the 5th Annual International Forum under the title "International Cybercrime Occurrence, Development and Prevention" held within the framework of the 16th German Congress on Crime Prevention in Oldenburg. The two-day forum was characterized by highly topical, interesting presentations and discussions as well as by an intense exchange between the experts attending the meeting.

Altogether six presentations given in the course of the two-day forum provided initial responses to the following questions:

1. What is the current situation with regard to the cybercrime phenomenon?
2. What trends and developments may be expected?
3. What countermeasures have to be taken in order to effectively combat cybercrime?

As the cybercrime phenomenon is very multifaceted, it was approached from equally different angles. The experts managed to highlight socio-scientific, legal, economic and criminological aspects.

The perspective of the German security authorities was illustrated by two officers of the *Bundeskriminalamt*, Helmut Ujen and Mirko Manske. They gave an outline of the criminological phenomenology, as far as it is perceived by the *Bundeskriminalamt*.

Frank Ackermann, representative of the *Eco-Verband der Deutschen Internetindustrie* (Association of the German Internet Industry), reported on interesting crime suppression approaches pursued by the economy and the cooperation between the economy and security authorities. Media consultant Frank Tentler informed the audience on the structures and the functioning of social networks, possible dangers and on the developments that are to be expected in this area.

From the perspective of the European Commission, the political level, Marc Arno Hartwig described possible measures against the dangers outlined. Finally, Cornelia Schild of the *Bundesamt für Sicherheit in der Informationstechnik* (Federal Office for Information Security) and Sven Karge of the *Eco-Verband* (Association of the German Internet Industry) supplied information about a public-private partnership successfully launched in the field of combating botnets.

---

[1]   Slightly revised version of the presentation given in Oldenburg on 31 May 2011.

"Using the Internet is like skating on natural ice: Sometimes you do not know how thick or thin the ice is. In some places, the ice is thin and skating is dangerous. Nevertheless skating is great fun." This is how a participant very aptly described the attractions and risks of the Internet.

The Internet gives impetus to social and economic development. It is a medium used for networking, accelerating and simplifying. It has become indispensable for a large number of daily activities. At the same time, we have to be aware of the threats posed by malfunctions and cybercrime. The growing possibilities of the digital world also imply an increase in the dangers involved.

1 Situation

1.1 Positive Aspects of the Internet – Social and Economic Potentials

The Internet offers enormous potential for social and economic developments at national and international level. More and more people in Germany have Internet access, with not only younger people having a share in this development but also older ones, i.e. almost 40 per cent of the people aged over 60 regularly use the Internet.[2]

There is no doubt that the Internet is an important element of today's society: To imagine not only the world of work, the education, trade and services sectors, but also social contacts, especially social networks, without the Internet is impossible. We all use the Internet for procedures like online banking, the tax declaration, which is submitted to the tax office preferably via the Internet, the registration of vehicles and so forth. Due to the mobility of the devices necessary to that end, not least due to the increasing dissemination of smart phones, the Internet can be used in nearly all places at any time. This means that the World Wide Web can be accessed from everywhere; people do no longer depend on fixed business hours, for example.

Nowadays, it is quite simple to establish new forms of communication; making and maintaining contacts is becoming easier, at least in technical terms. These developments are global trends. All of you know charts that show the share of Internet users in the populations of the individual countries in the world. Europe and the USA have an eye-catching appearance; the use of the Internet is widespread in these countries. But also on the African continent the number of Internet users is significantly increasing.

This is the "bright side" of the Internet, the facet that simplifies our lives and that is fun.

---

[2]   *Bundesverband Digitale Wirtschaft* (Federal Association of the Digital Economy): In the third quarter of 2010, 73.4 per cent of the German-speaking resident population in Germany aged over 14 used the Internet. Almost all 14 to 39-year-olds (well over 90 per cent) are present in the Internet, the 40 to 49-year-olds have a share of 86.3 per cent, the 50 to 59-year-olds of 73.2 per cent. Still more than one third of the persons aged over 60 (36.2 per cent) use the Internet.

1.2 The Dangers of the Internet – The Law Enforcement Situation

The focus of the discussions at the forum, however, was on the "dark side" of the Internet, which one participant defined as the "portals of threat". Danger lurks in all areas: social media, online banking, geodata, e-commerce. The lecturers stated that in many cases IT security is not included in the original programme architecture, but has to be added later on in a complex and costly procedure.

Cybercrime in part includes conventional forms of crime, which duplicate merely on the Internet. Therefore, the Internet on the one hand is a new instrument of crime. On the other hand, we are facing new types of crime phenomena which were previously non-existent in this form. The experts complained in particular about the lacking overview of these new phenomena.

In this connection, according to the experts, it is questionable to what extent the figures shown in the police crime statistics are valid. Might it be that business enterprises with their specific interests are behind the figures? What is the estimated number of undetected cases? The experts participating in the forum voiced doubts as regards the usability of these crime statistical data.

The police crime statistics show that cybercrime is one of the growth sectors of delinquency. A decrease is noted with regard to many other types of crime and case numbers in total. In contrast, the number of cybercrime cases recorded alone between 2009 and 2010 rose by approximately 20 per cent. Also with respect to the damage caused by cybercrime, increases by up to 50 or 60 per cent are noted. These figures are a matter of concern.

However, the figures mentioned above refer to recorded crimes only. How many offences are not reported to the law enforcement agencies, for example because private victims have no clue about their computers being part of a globally operating botnet? How many enterprises become aware of an attack but refrain from reporting it to the law enforcement agencies for fear of damage to their image?

One thing is for certain: The offenders 2.0 come from all traditional fields of crime known to the police and the judicial authorities. These offences involve organized crime, terrorism, child pornography, industrial espionage, fraud and also offences against state security and corruption offences. All this can be found on the Internet - there are, however, some new facets that also gave the participants of the forum food for thought. Phenomena such as the theft of digital identities, which the offenders use for shopping sprees on the World Wide Web, thus being able to cause considerable damage, are something to be seriously concerned about. Moreover, the possibility to create digital clones or - in other words - parallel identities, bears an enormous damage potential.

This is also true for the developments in the field of phishing. You all know this phenomenon, many of you received so-called phishing mails at some time or another: What was very clumsy when it started some years ago has meanwhile become more professional through corresponding social engineering applied by the offenders. Nowadays, you catch Trojans through so-called "drive-by infections". A supposedly non-compromised website, for example the website of the *Bundeskriminalamt* or the *Bundesamt für Sicherheit in der Informationstechnik,* might be a forged website that can hardly be distinguished from the genuine one and that infects your computer with a Trojan when website contents are retrieved.

Also classical forms of crime such as extortion, protection racketeering and extortion for ransom nowadays take place on the Internet. If we stick to the term, there is a mafia 2.0, which no longer robs banks somewhere but uses the opportunities provided by the Internet to approach enterprises and to threaten them with spam attacks. If the enterprises menaced in such a way do not take the threats seriously, their servers get flooded. The fact that enterprises are unavailable because their servers are being flooded may cause considerable losses. Corresponding cases have shown that the threat is associated with an actual damage that may cause significant problems for an enterprise, in some cases even for smaller countries.

One topic of the future, as was expressly emphasized by the experts, are mobile terminals. Many people already have such mobile terminals, which combine more and more functions. The consequence is that in the future mobile terminals will become the target of an increasing number of attacks, for example by botnets. This is certainly an issue that, under the aspect of prevention, should be in the focus of attention in the future.

In the meantime, an underground economy, a wide range of criminal products offered on the Internet, has developed. Digital identities, credit card data, Trojans or complete botnets can be acquired at relatively low cost, and on that basis considerable damage can be caused with relatively limited IT skills.

"That has been our depression day" - this is how one participant aptly described the first day of the 5th Annual International Forum. What action can or must be taken in the field of prevention? Are the instruments we have effective? What can we do when realizing that our own computers pose a potential threat? These were the questions we faced at the beginning of the second day.

2 Countermeasures – Players and Methods

The discussions on those involved in counteraction and on the methods used in this context focused on the following questions: What preventive countermeasures can we offer? What players and methods have been involved so far? Nearly all lecturers felt that, on the one hand, we are lucky to have a large number of different initiatives at national and international level - which in my opinion is an important message emanating from this year's Congress on Crime Prevention. Many actors are strongly committed to developing measures against cybercrime. However, according to the experts, there are some areas still requiring considerable effort to catch up. For example, with regard to "awareness", i.e. the technological and consciousness-related IT security, we have to take countermeasures as soon as ever possible. The gap between what is happening in the field of cybercrime and what we are doing to counter it must not widen.

2.1 Security Authorities

Since March this year, the Federal Government has pursued a common cyber security strategy. In this connection, the security authorities fulfil their traditional tasks involving law enforcement and aversion of danger. Employees from different fields of work, such as scientists, technicians, police officers and other experts work together in the security authorities every day. In the field of traditional police repression, the police and judicial authorities, among other things, face the challenge to find solutions to the question of how to secure traces on the Internet in such a way that they may be used as evidence in court later on. A further challenge is posed by the large data volumes that have to be analysed in connection with investigative proceedings.

The experts participating in the forum pointed to the need to intensely deal with future developments. Due to the dynamics inherent in cybercrime we are well-advised to use procedures such as scenario planning for identifying probable future developments. This also involves a monitoring system that functions properly. Instead of trying to catch up with developments, a situation we complained about, we must be acting with an eye to the future. Examples of recent developments are modern payment systems such as WebMoney or Ukash. Moreover, the experts addressed issues that (still) appear futuristic, e.g. "digital camouflage", which is currently under development and can be used for covering up criminal activity.

2.2 Economy and Associations

Representatives of the economic sector and the associations pointed to the different platforms and forms of cooperation that have so far been established for preventive purposes. These include, on the one hand, activities by the economic sector in its specific spheres of activity. On the other hand, examples were given in which prevention programmes carried out by other actors, such as schools especially at local level, are supported by commercial enterprises and associations.

2.3 Users

It is also the users who are required to act accordingly and who have to consider themselves to be central elements of the security structure. The awareness of and sensitivity for the dangers of the Internet, have to be strengthened. In view of the fact that even antivirus software installed on the computer cannot provide complete protection and is able to identify only a part of the viruses currently on the market, the users have a special responsibility.

2.4 Public-Private Partnership

The issue of public-private partnership was presented on the basis of a current example, the Anti-Botnet Consultancy Centre. The Anti-Botnet Consultancy Centre is a cooperation project between the *Bundesamt für Sicherheit in der Informationstechnik* and the *Verband der deutschen Internetwirtschaft*. Internet service providers and providers of anti-virus software are also involved in this close cooperation. It is remarkable that this cooperation project does not restrict itself to being just a strategic advisory body but that concrete advice is offered to enterprises or individual persons affected by a botnet attack. The experts asserted that, if necessary, call centre employees would go through a work plan item by item together with the caller in order to ultimately remove the Trojan responsible for integrating the computer into the botnet from the computer.

3 Conclusions

As indicated several times before, many aspects remain yet to be settled in the dynamic field of cybercrime. The knowledge of the phenomenon is in part not very profound. Awareness of the impending threats has to be strengthened. What conclusions can be drawn from the lectures and discussions especially in terms of prevention?

3.1 Extension of Existing Cooperations

Many players have already been active in the field of cybercrime prevention. Existing cooperations have to be extended and strengthened. Especially in the field of prevention there still is potential for optimisation.

3.2 Keeping up with the Dynamics of Development

According to the experts, the developmental dynamics of the Internet and hence also of cybercrime will not diminish. Professor Potja appropriately stated that in the past those involved in technological innovation had still had much time to think about solutions to problems. The experts at the forum were unanimous that this time is no longer available. We must react more quickly and intensify our preventive effort.

3.3 Strengthening Research Activities

Cybercrime-related research activities must be pushed ahead. The phenomenological knowledge on what is happening on the Internet is to be improved. It is a task area of classical criminology to learn more about the manifestations and the quantitative dimension of cybercrime. Furthermore, clearing up undetected crimes also counts among the classical social science research and is an area that has to be tackled. On the other hand, it is necessary to improve technological research with a view to preventing opportunities to commit offences on the Internet and especially with a view to stepping up IT security. This is the only way we can obtain more information on risks as well as on crime, victim and offender structures.

3.4 Suppression of Cybercrime as a Task for the Whole of Society

The fight against cybercrime is a task to be tackled by the whole of society. The experts' lectures made clear that cybercrime is a classical cross-sectoral issue. As a consequence, this means that we have to develop strategies at interdepartmental level. We all must assume our share of obligation in the preventive value chain from private users to enterprises and state actors.

3.5 Intensification of the Social Discourse

In the opinion of the experts, the social discourse on what should take place on the Internet and what not, has to be intensified.

"Don't be stupid", that is the simple formula for prevention. But is this sufficient or do we need more regimentation? What level of freedom should there be on the Internet? What role do the individual actors play? Are pure Internet ethics sufficient, which the users themselves develop for all intents and purposes, or do we need more state regulation? The World Wide Web is, one the one hand, global. However, a glance at the European countries alone shows that they in part have very different views regarding the extent to which the state should intervene. The discussion on the Act to Impede Access to Child Pornography Content in Communication Networks, which was introduced in Germany and repealed afterwards, is a good example for illustrating the problem.

3.6 Strengthening Media Competence

For the purpose of making a universal prevention approach, media competence must be broadened and promoted in all areas of society. Information and preventive work in respect of children must start as soon as they touch a device connected with the Internet for the first time. At this point, specific education and awareness production must begin.

3.7 New Forms of Cooperation between Private and Public Actors

We must try out new forms of cooperation between private and public actors, both at national and international level. There are many existing or developing forms of cooperation on a local, national and international scale. These have to be tested further and expanded. As far as possible, they have to be scientifically supported in some cases in order to enable us to assess how these networks can be organized in an effective manner.

3.8 Extension of Individual Offers of Assistance

In the opinion of the experts, the individual offers of assistance are to be expanded. The Anti-Botnet Consultancy Centre, jointly run by a public authority and an association, is a good example. Forum attendants compared it with the burglary prevention advice services provided by the police. This means that, according to the experts, traditional areas of crime, for which the police have established an ample advice system, have to be extended to cybercrime. A government agency is required which people can call for advice.

3.9 Adaptation of Prevention Methods

Our prevention methods have to be adapted. The prevention actors need a new specific social engineering, they need to know how to reach the respective target groups. "Listen, Learn and Lead", these catchwords describe how actors in the end assume leading roles in terms of prevention activities. Thus, we have somewhat called into question one point of Wiebke Steffen's presentation yesterday: Are the methods of the analog world transferable to the digital world? Taking into account the results of our forum this is questionable, which consequently means that specific instruments will have to be developed.

3.10 Provision of Resources

Sufficient resources are to be made available for countermeasures and prevention. This is not surprising. In the final analysis, one of the pleasant side effects of public-private partnership is that the economic sector bears part of the costs and that cooperations are set up, by means of which training measures can be financed.

These are the essential findings of the 5th Annual International Forum at the 16th German Congress on Crime Prevention.

I would like to take this opportunity to thank all lecturers for their excellent presentations and the participants in the discussions for their contributions. Thank you very much for an informative and goal-oriented forum.

Oldenburg Declaration of the 16th German Congress on Crime Prevention

New Worlds of Media – Challenges for the Prevention of Crime?

New media worlds – these refer to digital worlds that have been existence since the turn of the century and have fundamentally changed both social life and the life of each individual. The new - digital – media, primarily the Internet and mobile phones, have in the meantime become commonplace, and one can no longer imagine life without them.

In 2010, virtually 50 million people, or 70% of the German-speaking population from the age of 14 and older were online; 100% of the younger age groups ranging from 14 to 29 years surf on the Internet, and this market is also completely satiated with regard to mobile phones. It is especially the older generations that are not online, whereat the "digital trench" is currently at about 65 years of age.

The **Internet,** which is the basic medium of the digitalised world, has evolved to become a universal and multi-functional communication medium for information and entertainment, providing us with texts, (moving) images and sounds. Never before has one single medium attained such a high rate of dissemination in such as short space of time of not even quite two decades.

Without a doubt, the new digital media do offer many positive fields of application, but they also entail problematic areas, risks and dangers, right up to criminality. Hence, the digital media also provide challenges in the field of crime prevention.

For this reason, the 16th German Congress on Crime Prevention has made the new worlds of media its topic of focus. On the basis of the expertise elaborated by Dr. Wiebke Steffen "New Worlds of Media – Challenges for the Prevention of Crime?" the German Congress on Crime Prevention and its conference partners, the DBH-Bildungswerk (Educational Society), Landespräventionsrat Niedersachsen (LPR) (State Prevention Council of Lower Saxony), Polizeiliche Kriminalprävention der Länder und des Bundes (Police Crime Prevention of the States and the Federation), (ProPK), Präventionsrat Oldenburg (Prevention Council Oldenburg) (PRO), Stiftung Deutsches Forum für Kriminalprävention (Foundation German Forum for the Prevention of Crime) (DFK), and WEISSER RING, have issued the following **"Oldenburg Declaration".**

The "digital revolution" not only harbours great potential, it also entails dangers and risks

As is the case in the analogue world, infringement of laws, violations of rules, right up to criminal acts, also occur in the digital world. In principle, all the dangers of criminality which exist outside of the Internet are now in the Internet too. In addition, the internet makes possible or even encourages certain problematic modes of conduct that are detrimental in one way or another. Moreover, such conduct can gain in explosiveness due to the framework conditions typical of the Internet.

Particularly noteworthy in this regard are, e.g. the capacity for automation as well as the disappearance of spatial barriers; the anonymity; the rapid dissemination of the contents; the ability to copy and proliferate information, as well as the (permanent) storage thereof ("the Internet doesn't forget").

All in all, the potential for danger and damage, as made possible by cyber-crime, is high and what is more, it is clearly on the rise. This is even further facilitated by the fact that the perpetrators rapidly adapt to the technical conditions and display enormous innovative capacity.

*The **German Congress on Crime Prevention** emphatically urges that the Internet not be allowed to become a sphere in which there are no laws. A balance has to be found between the right to freedom of information and opinion on the one hand, and the justified protection of the rights of users on the other. Especially as there is a large economic and political interest in participating in the utilisation of digital media and providing free unimpeded access to the Internet, the internet users must be able to rely on the fact that the constitutional state will establish the framework conditions that ensure the privacy and integrity of IT-based systems.*

Independently of this, as in the past, everything possible must be undertaken to educate the internet users – and this includes all user groups – about the possible repercussions of increasing online crime. In this regard, there is a particular need to inform them about identity theft. In addition, it is important to further sensitize them regarding the risks and provide them with sensible protective measures. Due to the limited efficiency of (safety-relevant) technical approaches and countermeasures – especially in terms of time considerations – human behaviour, as an important crimogenic factor, has to be considered and placed at the centre of focus, in conjunction with delinquency on the Internet.

Very little sound knowledge regarding the risk and perils of digital media

The warnings issued regarding the virtually unrestricted inducements and possibilities offered by the Internet, especially in respect of its inappropriate use, stand in stark contrast to the actual knowledge about the risks and dangers associated with the Internet. On the one hand, this possibly is due to the large proportion of unreported cases, which might be even larger than that of "analogue" crime. On the other hand, however, this also is due to the novelty of numerous perils, in the sense of a general – or also specific, possibly age-specific – threat, as well as the rapid development of the digital media and the speedy changes in usage and user behaviour.

Numerous media offers have been on the "market" for too short a time to assess their medium- or even long-term effects. There are no extensive, representative criminological studies or long-term panel and longitudinal investigative studies. The emotional intensity of the debate is entirely disproportionate to actual knowledge about the risks and their possible (lasting) effects.

*The **German Congress on Crime Prevention** considers it extremely important to conduct extensive, broadly-based and representative criminological studies as well as long-term panel and longitudinal investigative studies. An evidence-based criminal policy requires a sufficiently reliable statistical basis, which urgently has to be created. In so doing, it has to be ascertained whether the investigation of new media does not also necessitate the development of new (empirical) methods and approaches.*

The Internet attracts a high level of attention as a risk-factor for adolescents

In the perception of the general public, the Internet poses a particularly great threat for adolescents. These risks principally include their extreme carelessness in dealing with personal information, the impacts of violence-related content and in particular the effect of violent computer games on their own behavioural patterns. Furthermore, risks are also seen in excessive media consumption, right up to computer addiction; confrontation with pornography and sexual harassment, politically motivated crime and extremism, cyber-mobbing and cyber-bullying, as well as the infringements of personality rights and copyright.

However, to date, there still is hardly any reliable information on how many adolescents actually have already come into contact with problematic contents, and which impacts these contents have had on them (or also could possibly have on them), or how frequently and how long the young adults display risky, excessively careless or even criminally-relevant behaviour.

*In the course of the "digital-media risk discussion", the **German Congress on Crime Prevention** expressly warns against repeating the pitfalls and arguments of "conventional" medial and criminal-political discussions regarding juvenile delinquency and endangerment of youth. It would be wrong to assume that the problems with digital media are primarily to be found among "young adults", to regard young adults as having fewer standards and acting more unscrupulously than the adult generation or to fear that "they could stay the way they are now".*

*The **German Congress on Crime Prevention** expressly points out that the majority of young adults obviously do know how to deal with the computer and also do find the balance between computer and other activities – as is the case in the analogue world, too, where most of the adolescents are generally able to face the challenges posed, without any particularly conspicuous behaviour and are successful at finding their way in the world (Wiesbaden Declaration of the 12th German Congress on Crime Prevention).*

*For the **German Congress on Crime Prevention**, there is no reason to assume that "digital" juvenile delinquency and the endangerment of youth are subject to different pre-conditions and regularities than "analogue" juvenile delinquency. That is why juvenile delinquency should be regarded and evaluated with a sense of proportion in both the cyber and analogue worlds.*

*Regardless of the aforementioned, the **German Congress on Crime Prevention** does deem it necessary to address the general public's concerns about the media competence of the younger generation, as well as the fears regarding the risks and dangers on the Internet and the mistrust toward the younger generation's "digital" behaviour.*

There is an urgent need to conduct long-term criminological surveys pertaining to the media and communication behaviour of young adults. In so doing, particular attention has to be paid to the "motives for using the Internet" and "individual perceptual processes".

Crime prevention in the digital world: empowering people, creating protective mechanisms

Assuming the premise that the decisive – constitutive - feature for the prevention of crime is also given in the digital world; that there is a clear understanding on what is to be considered "permitted and not-permitted" or "desirable and non-desirable"; assuming that the digital world does not claim to be a law-free zone, then crime prevention can pursue the following three primary strategies in order to prevent or mitigate the potential dangers and risks: crime prevention by means of statutory and (safety-relevant) technical arrangement, measures and recommendations; crime prevention by means of protecting minors in the media; and crime prevention by means of media competence.

*Even though the internet users and their behavioural patterns are of vital importance for the effect and effectivity of crime prevention efforts and measures, the **German Congress on Crime Prevention** expressly demands that crime prevention efforts be strengthened by means of statutory as well as technical measures for security and recommendations, and not minimised. Both politics and the economy must be aware of their responsibility for protecting the users, their trust in the security of the network, and their personality rights and data, and act accordingly. The government has the task of protecting the Internet as a free and liberal medium; the citizens have to be able to rely on the fact that the constitutional state will establish the framework conditions that will guarantee the privacy and integrity of IT-based systems. In particular, the efforts of the police for crime prevention are to be extended and strengthened, with the objectives of improving the security of users in handling the new media; informing them of the dangers and criminal offences, and cooperating with other actors working in this field.*

As a basic principle, the **German Congress on Crime Prevention** *does deem the existing German statutory stipulations for the protection of minors in the media to be sufficient for protecting them against problematic content, particularly in light of the fact that the influence of many parents on the media behaviour of their children is declining or, perhaps more exactly, quite a number of parents are tending to give up the efforts of controlling this, as they do not have the knowledge to deal with new media.*

This is another reason why the **German Congress on Crime Prevention** *considers it necessary to further improve the conditions for risk management in the protection of minors.*

The **German Congress on Crime Prevention** *welcomes all efforts aimed at further improving the media competence of all users of digital media, so that they can utilise the opportunities these media offer, yet at the same time avoid the potential pitfalls. With regard to the media competence of children and adolescents, the* **German Congress on Crime Prevention** *demands that the world should also respect their manner of using the media and their mode of expressing themselves within this media, and it should be acknowledged that by no means are they helpless in dealing with this media and do need the freedom that this digital world can offer them. Regardless of this, they also need support. As it cannot be assumed that this support can be provided by the parents in all cases, it is especially the schools that need to take on this task of imparting media competence. The German Congress on Crime Prevention demands that schools and teachers be educated accordingly, so that they can accompany the process of integrating the digital media into the everyday life at school in an evaluating manner.*

With regard to the challenges for crime prevention, the 16th German Congress on Crime Prevention refers to the discussions of the 12th, 13th, 14th and 15th German Congresses on Crime Prevention, the demands and appeals of the "Wiesbaden Declaration", the "Leipzig Declaration", the "Hanover Declaration" as well as the "Berlin Declaration"

Their topicality and urgency still remain undiminished to this very day.

Oldenburg, 31 May 2011

Program of the 4th Annual International Forum

The 4th Annual International Forum presents in special cooperation with the
General Assembly 2010 of the European Forum for Urban Safety (EFUS):
How cities reconcile security and fundamental rights
International Congress Centrum (ICC) Berlin

Monday, May 10th 2010

9:00 - 10:30
Entrance Hall

Arrival of the international Guests
(A special check-in counter is at the disposal of our international guests)

11:00 - 12:30
Hall 1

Opening Plenum of the German Congress on Crime Prevention
(German with interpretation into English, French, Italian and Spanish)

Welcome by the Executive Director of the German Congress on Crime Prevention
Erich Marks

Welcoming address by the minister of the interior and sport of the State of Berlin
Dr. Ehrhart Körting

Welcoming address by the President of the German Foundation of the prevention of Crime (DVS)
Professor Dr. Hans-Jürgen Kerner

Introduction by the author of the report for 15th German Congress on Crime Prevention
Dr. Wiebke Steffen
Bavarian State Investigation Bureau

Welcoming address by the director for security of the Deutsche Bahn Group
Professor Gerd Neubeck

Was shapes us, knowledge or experiences?
Professor Dr. Gerald Hüther
Head of the joint neurobiological prevention research at the universities of Göttingen, Mannheim and Heidelberg

Artistic contributions:
CABUWAZI: Children and Youth Circus
Artistic director: Fabian Gröger
„With Music against violence" Orchestra of the primary school Fritzlar-Homberg,
Director: Angelika Maillard-Städter

12:30 - 13:30
GCOCP Catering Area

Opportunity for Lunch

The 4th Annual International Forum presents in special cooperation with the
General Assembly 2010 of the European Forum for Urban Safety (EFUS):
How cities reconcile security and fundamental rights
International Congress Centrum (ICC) Berlin

13:30 - 15:00
Hall 7

Opening session:
Security and Freedom in a new European and international context
(Interpretation between English, French, German, Italian and Spanish)

Chair: Michel Marcus, Executive Director EFUS

Welcome and introduction
Erich Marks, Director of the Annual International Forum and Secretary of the Executive Committee of ICPC
Prof. Dr. Hans-Jürgen Kerner, President of the GCOCP and the German Foundation for Crime Prevention
Alberto Juan Belloch Julbe, Mayor of Zaragossa and President of the EFUS

Convincing governments to invest in prevention - reducing crime protecting rights
Prof. Dr. Irvin Waller, Professor for Criminology, University of Ottawa

The international context including the action plan of the 12th UN Congress on Crime Prevention
Dr. Paula Miraglia, Director General of the International Centre for the Prevention of Crime Montreal

Ensuring security and fundamental rights in urban settings
Dr. Alexander Butchart, World Health Organization

15:30 - 16:45
Hall 7

Ensuring security and fundamental rights in the context of immigrant societies
(Interpretation between English, French, German, Italian and Spanish)

The exeperiences of Modena and Italy
Giorgio PIGHI, Mayor of Modena and president of the Italian Forum for Urban Safety (tbc)

The exeperiences of Molenbeek-Saint-Jean and Belgium
Philippe MOUREAUX, Maire de Molenbeek-Saint-Jean and President of the Belgian Forum for Urban Safety (tbc)

How the UK cities manage the different issues linked to immigration in the context of security and fundamental rights.
Jane Mowat, President of the National Community Safety Network (NCSN) (tbc)

German examples: 'Violence Prevention Network' and 'Cultures Interactive', Berlin
PD Dr. Harald Weilnböck (Berlin / Zürich)

Discussion

The 4th Annual International Forum presents in special cooperation with the
General Assembly 2010 of the European Forum for Urban Safety (EFUS):
How cities reconcile security and fundamental rights
International Congress Centrum (ICC) Berlin

17:00 - 18:30
Hall 7

Security technology supporting fundamental rights?
(Interpretation between English, French, German, Italian and Spanish)

The challenge of new technologies for the protection of fundamental rights and privacy
Peter Schaar, Federal Commissioner for Data Protection and Freedom of Information (tbc)

New security technology, democracy, privacy and effective crime prevention
Peter Squires, Professor for Criminology and Politics, University Brighton (tbc)

How to use social network for crime prevention
Johanna Seppälä, City of Helsinki

New technologies to foster citizen participation and social cohesion
Cécile Arches, City of Issy-les-Moulineaux

Discussion

18:30
Hall 2

Evening Reception of the GCOCP

The 4th Annual International Forum presents in special cooperation with the
General Assembly 2010 of the European Forum for Urban Safety (EFUS):
How cities reconcile security and fundamental rights
International Congress Centrum (ICC) Berlin

Tuesday, May 11. 2010

9:00 - 10:30
Hall 7

Involvement of citizens and civil society in crime prevention
(Interpretation between English, French, German, Italian and Spanish)

Chair: Dr. Marc Coester, Coordinator International Affairs for the GCOCP

Citizen's participation in crime prevention
Prof. Dr. Paul Ekblom, Professor of Design Against Crime, University of the Arts London

**Activating community coalitions for effective prevention planning:
the Communities That Care approach**
Dr. Sabrina Oesterle, Social Development Research Group, University of Washington, Seattle

The citizen participation project "FONDACA" in Genoa
Francesco Scidone, Councillor in charge of security and prevention of the city of Genoa (tbc)

Overview of Violence Prevention in Berlin
Stephan Voß, Crime Prevention Council of the state of Berlin (Landeskommission Berlin gegen Gewalt)

Discussion

11:00 - 12:30
Hall 7

Closing session:
How do the new European and international policies respond to local crime prevention issues? Reconciling security and fundamental rights - the mission of (D)EFUS
(Interpretation between English, French, German, Italian and Spanish)

Chair: Michel Marcus, Executive Director EFUS

The vision of the European Parliament for crime prevention and the field of security and freedom
Juan Fernando Lopez Aguilar, Member of the European Parliament, President of the Committee on Civil Liberties, Justice and Home Affairs (LIBE) (tbc)

The action plan to implement the Stockholm programme on justice, freedom and security (2009-2014)
N.N., EU Crime Prevention Network (EUCPN)

A Forum for German and European exchanges on human-rights based crime prevention: (D)EFUS
Erich Marks, Managing Director of the GCOCP and member of the EFUS Executive Committee
Dr. Martin Schairer, Mayor in charge of security and order, Stuttgart and member of the EFUS Executive Committee

Conclusions
Alberto Juan Belloch Julbe, Mayor of Zaragossa and President of the EFUS
Guilherme PINTO, Mayor of Matosinhos and president of the Portuguese Forum for Urban Safety
Pierre COHEN, President of the Toulouse metropolitan area

Discussion

The 4th Annual International Forum presents in special cooperation with the
General Assembly 2010 of the European Forum for Urban Safety (EFUS):
How cities reconcile security and fundamental rights
International Congress Centrum (ICC) Berlin

12:30 - 13:30
GCOCP Catering Area
Opportunity for Lunch

A special lunch for EFUS members is provided in the Pullman Lounge

13:30 - 16:30
Hall 7

Internal part of the EFUS General Assembly
(closed shop only for EFUS members)

13:30 - 15:00
Exhibition of the GCOCP
Meeting at the poster stands

Walk over the exhibition

Guided and interpreted visits are proposed for international participants, which are not members of EFUS to discover the exhibition of the German Congress on Crime prevention, where more than 200 institutions and projects present their work in the area of crime prevention. The visit will be organised in groups (English and other languages if necessary). Guide and interpreter will allow participants to get in contact with the German crime prevention scene.

15:00 - 16:00
Hall 3
Closing Plenum of the GCOCP
(German with interpretation into English)

Closing speech of the president of the GCOCP
Professor Dr. Hans-Jürgen Kerner
University of Tübingen

„Berlin Declaration" of the 15th German Congress on Crime Prevention
Dr. Wiebke Steffen
Bavarian State Investigation Bureau

Cradle to Cradle and the prevention of environmental crime
Professor Dr. Michael Braungart
Erasmus-University Rotterdam, Executive Director of „ EPEA International Environmental Research" Hamburg,
Scientific Director of the Hamburg Environmental Institute

Outlook and closing address
Erich Marks
Executive Director of the German Congress on Crime Prevention

Finale:
Choir of the Lessing High School Berlin
IesSINGersTC, Conductor: Thomas Carl

Program of the 5th Annual International Forum

The 5th Annual International Forum presents in special cooperation with the
Federal Criminal Police Office as well as the Federal Office for Information Security:
International Cybercrime – Occurrence, Development, Prevention
Weser Ems Halle, Oldenburg

Bundeskriminalamt

Bundesamt
für Sicherheit in der
Informationstechnik

Monday, May 30th 2011

9:00 - 10:30
Entrance Hall

Arrival of the international Guests
(A special check-in counter is at the disposal of our international guests)

11:00 - 12:30
Congress Hall

Opening Plenum of the German Congress on Crime Prevention
(German with interpretation into English)

Welcome by the Executive Director of the German Congress on Crime Prevention
Erich Marks
German Congress on Crime Prevention

Welcoming address
David McAllister
Prime Minister of the Federal State of Lower Saxony

Welcoming address
Professor Dr. Gerd Schwandner
Lord Mayor of the City of Oldenburg

Welcoming address
Professor Dr. Ilsu Kim
President of the Korean Institute of Criminology

Welcome address
Jan Janssen
Bishop of the Protestant-Lutheran Church Oldenburg

Remarks about the main topic of the congress "New Media World – Challenge for Crime Prevention"
Dr. Wiebke Steffen
Author of the Report for the Congress

Keynote Speech
Professor Dr. Elisabeth Pott
Head of the Federal Centre for Health Education

12:30 - 14:00
GCOCP Catering Area

Opportunity for Lunch

The 5th Annual International Forum presents in special cooperation with the
Federal Criminal Police Office as well as the Federal Office for Information Security:
International Cybercrime – Occurrence, Development, Prevention
Weser Ems Halle, Oldenburg

14:00 - 15:00
Hall 2

Opening session of the Annual International Forum:
International Cybercrime – Occurrence, Development, Prevention

Chair:
Dr. Marc Coester (German Congress on Crime Prevention)

New Technologies and Cybercrime
Helmut Ujen
Federal Criminal Police Office, KI 2

Discussion

15:30 - 16:30
Hall 2

International Cybercrime: Fundamentals of Security

Chair:
Dr. Marc Coester (GCOCP)

The current level of threat concerning Malware and digital Identity Theft
Mirko Manske
Federal Criminal Police Office

Discussion

17:00 - 18:00
Hall 2

International Cybercrime: Fundamentals of Security

Chair:
Dr. Burkhard Hasenpusch (Crime Prevention Council Lower Saxony)

Media Security – Who is Responsible?
Frank Ackermann
eco - Association of the German Internet Industry

Discussion

18:30
Congress Hall

Evening Reception of the GCOCP

The 5th Annual International Forum presents in special cooperation with the
Federal Criminal Police Office as well as the Federal Office for Information Security:
International Cybercrime – Occurrence, Development, Prevention
Weser Ems Halle, Oldenburg

Tuesday, May 31. 2011

9:00 - 10:00
Hall 2
International Cybercrime: Effects for Citizens

Chair:
Dr. Marc Coester (GCOCP)

Social Networks and their Danger
Frank Tentler
Media Consultant

Discussion

10:30 - 11:30
Hall 2

International Cybercrime: Prevention and Cooperation

Chair:
Dr. Marc Coester (GCOCP)

Cybercrime Prevention – A European solution?
Marc Arno Hartwig
European Commission
Directorate-General Home Affairs (DG HOME)

Discussion

11:30 - 12:30
GCOCP Catering Area
Opportunity for Lunch

12:30 - 13:30
Hall 2

International Cybercrime: Prevention and Cooperation

Chair:
Dr. Marc Coester (GCOCP)

The Anti-Botnet Advisory Centre
Cornelia Schildt
Federal Office for Information Security
Sven Karge
eco - Association of the German Internet Industry

Discussion

The 5th Annual International Forum presents in special cooperation with the
Federal Criminal Police Office as well as the Federal Office for Information Security:
International Cybercrime – Occurrence, Development, Prevention
Weser Ems Halle, Oldenburg

Plenum of the German Congress on Crime Prevention
(German with interpretation into English)
Congress Hall

14:00 - 14:30
International Cybercrime: Results from the Annual International Forum
Prof. Dr. Jürgen Stock
Vice President of the Federal Criminal Police Office

14:30 - 14:45
The „Oldenburg Declaration" from the German Congress on Crime Prevention
Dr. Wiebke Steffen
Author of the Report for the Congress

14:45 - 15:00
Results from the congress
Prof. Dr. Hans-Jürgen Kerner
Congress President

15:00 - 15:50
New Media, Values Education, Behavior, Control
Prof. Dr. Dr. Manfred Spitzer
University Hospital Ulm

15:50 - 16:00
Outlook and closing address
Erich Marks
Executive Director of the German Congress on Crime Prevention

Authors

Paul Ekblom
Central Saint Martins College of Art & Design, London, UK

Wiebke Steffen
German Congress on Crime Prevention, Heiligenberg, Germany

Jürgen Stock
Bundeskriminalamt, Wiesbaden, Germany

Irvin Waller
University of Ottawa, Canada

Harald Weilnböck
Violence Prevention Network e. V. and Cultures Interactive e. V., Berlin, Germany